Jesus

The Same Yesterday, Today & Forever

Shirley Hall

authorHOUSE®

AuthorHouse™
1663 Liberty Drive
Bloomington, IN 47403
www.authorhouse.com
Phone: 1-800-839-8640

First published by AuthorHouse   7/8/2010

ISBN: 978-1-4520-1154-7 (e)
ISBN: 978-1-4520-1153-0 (sc)

Library of Congress Control Number: 2010904928

Printed in the United States of America
Bloomington, Indiana

This book is printed on acid-free paper.

Thanks to the Greatest Teacher, Jesus!
Thanks to a Great Friend, Mom!

Contents

Chapter 1
God of the Bible

There are many people much more qualified to write books than I, yet I find myself in this place again. I have this strong desire to go off and learn how to take on this project of writing a book, but, I know the Lord wants me to do this by being led by His spirit. I feel completely inadequate, however; I must be obedient to this present call on my life. He says I am a book writer so I have to agree by faith and watch him make me into an author. This has not been an easy task, just necessary for obedience! So now, once again, I get over myself and move onward.

God has spoken to many people to write down His affairs. Throughout the Bible He tells them to write visions, dreams and His words. He tells Habakkuk to write the vision so that people may run with it. John is commanded to write to tell of the end times. Many people were commanded to record different things for the Lord throughout the Bible. God Himself, wrote the law on tablets and He writes His Word upon our hearts. Even today people record poetry, prayers, songs, visions and dreams that are inspired by the Holy Spirit. In recent days, the Lord spoke these words, "Start Assembling". He wants us to start bringing together all the things He has been giving us. Assembling means, an act of fitting together of parts to form a complete unit. Many of us are sitting on a gold mine of riches that the Lord has imparted to us in the realm of giftings, by His Spirit. After the Lord spoke these two words I then had a vision. I saw many books flying through the air in every direction going throughout the earth. Are you one of these people sitting on a gold mine and not even realizing it, like me?

> *Isaiah 30:8(NKJV) Now go, write it before them on a tablet, And note it on a scroll, That it may be for time to come, Forever and ever: :*
> *Jeremiah 30:1-2(NKJV) The word that came to Jeremiah from the Lord, saying,*
> *"Thus speaks the Lord God of Israel, saying: 'Write in a book for yourself all the words that I have spoken to you.*
> *Habakkuk 2:2(NKJV) Then the Lord answered me and said: "Write the vision And make it plain on tablets, That he may run who reads it.*

I have been recording in my journals for many years and I try to write down every vision and dream because I think it is important. The key is knowing what to do with them afterward. The Holy Spirit will direct all of us as we are faithful in the first step of recording the Word of the Lord. I have a close friend that has recorded her prayers for years. Like me, she didn't really question why she was recording all these things. Now the Lord has directed her to begin a devotional book. I often thought, "How could a person record their prayers?" When she read them to me I recognized the anointing on them, so therefore, this task the Lord called her to does not surprise me. I didn't have a clue why I recorded everything. I knew according to the scripture that God's Words could be stolen so this was good enough reason to record all that He spoke and all that He revealed.

> *Matthew 13:22(NKJV) Now he who received seed among the thorns is he who hears the word, and the cares of this world and the deceitfulness of riches choke the word, and he becomes unfruitful.*

As God gives us His Word we must record it because you never know what He will want you to do with it later. Recording what the Lord reveals helps in sharing with others at times of relevancy. He has had me write curriculum and now He is having me write books. He has just told me to write another book which will include many dreams and visions to make a devotional book. He has given me the title "Praying

Through the Eyes of the Spirit." All the recording of what He has said, while journaling, is at my fingertips. I've had a stack of visions in my file cabinet for years. I had no idea that they would be used for anything except for a source for prayer or for memory purposes. If you are gathering words of the Lord, get ready! For there might come some surprising requests from the Lord. Once the Lord said I would stack the journals on my head and they would reach the ceiling. I truly thought that was funny and definitely exciting! Just the other day I read in one of my more recent journals. I was so blessed, once again, because He said that the journals were also going to be placed beneath my feet and they would act as stepping stones for days ahead. It rings truer today than my understanding was on that day. Looking back, I am a witness to many promises being fulfilled. I have been Amazed at what He has been bringing out of all those journals. When He gives, He has the end in mind and is looking for something to be produced out of it. I think of the parable of the talents where the good and faithful servants bring back increase.

Matthew 25:20-21(NKJV) *"So he who had received five talents came and brought five other talents, saying, 'Lord, you delivered to me five talents; look, I have gained five more talents besides them.' His lord said to him, 'Well done, good and faithful servant; you were faithful over a few things, I will make you ruler over many things. Enter into the joy of your lord.'*

He is always looking for the increase because it is His way. His kingdom and all that is in it ever increases upon this earth. He is a God of increase!

By looking back on the twenty three years of my life with the Lord I have come to the conclusion that nothing else will do when making decisions, except making decisions through Him and to do what He asks. I take pleasure in doing His will because I see nothing but increase when I follow His plan. He is truly faithful and can make something out of very little. Look how he brought increase from the two fish and five loaves of bread. He fed <u>five thousand people</u>. That's the kind of God we serve. Can you imagine what kind of increase He can bring by using all of us in the body of Christ? He used a little boy in that parable.

Imagine if we all could be there, our hands upheld with our little pieces of bread making ourselves available. Once we avail ourselves, He does the rest. I have no reservations in saying that I love everything about the Lord. I love the message He sent for mankind, I love his ways, I love what He speaks and I love His personality. I am always intrigued by what He does, what He says by His Holy Spirit, and I am always excited to enter each new adventure with Him. One thing I have found over the last twenty three years is that...

Jesus is the same Yesterday, Today and Forever.

From the very beginning, I saw an unbreakable tie to what He was doing in my life compared to what He did in other people's lives in the Bible. I am a witness and a testimony of the living Bible. We all are if we allow Him to move through us. I recognized how He related to people, how He spoke to people and I saw a strong correlation in my own relationship with Him. Of course there is just a bit of a time frame difference, like two thousand years! After seeing how Jesus has related to me and then seeing how He related to people in the Bible, I realized that there is nothing new under the sun. I will say, that I questioned why people dismissed the "Jesus of the Bible". It seemed that most of us lived a "good life" as Christians but, we seemed to be lacking the power that it so readily portrayed in the Word. I finally came to the conclusion that many of us were not representing Christ as he truly is. Of course, I stand before you just as guilty

Ecclesiastes 1:9(NKJV) That which has been is what will be, That which is done is what will be done, And there is nothing new under the sun.

I received the baptism of the Holy Spirit a couple of weeks after I received Christ in February of 1984. Yes, I was so excited when I got saved that I literally could not keep my feet on the ground. When I was filled with the Holy Spirit a power came over me which shook me from my head to my toes. Immediately I began speaking in tongues. As this gift was released through me it seemed very potent. I was astonished at the sound of the words that flowed through me, being a person never learning a foreign language. However, with a certainty I recognized the validity of its authenticity. I had never heard of such a thing in all my life except that in previous days I had overheard my mother praying quietly at the altar in her heavenly language. I remember thinking how sweet it sounded. Consequently, in the days to follow, after I received that infilling, I began to investigate in that new book, the Bible, for something to confirm that this was as miraculous as it felt. Sure enough, *there it was*! I was awed by the fact that a very similar experience was recorded in a book which was written over two thousand years ago. That truly amazed me! Yet, I continually find people rejecting the infilling and rejecting the signs that follow. We have to be open to everything the Bible speaks about because that is what God's kingdom entails. As we receive Him for who He is, we will open doors to the greatest riches on earth. These things are what people desire. Our creator placed those desires within us. There is something inside us that desires the miraculous, BECAUSE HE IS A MIRACULOUS GOD!

Acts 19:2(NKJV) he said to them, "Did you receive the Holy Spirit when you believed?" So they said to him, "We have not so much as heard whether there is a Holy Spirit."

This initial encounter with the Lord struck me **so hard** and impacted me so greatly that it ROCK SOLIDLY solidified my being born again and being Spirit-filled. I needed something to shake me at that time of my life. When I read about the entire encounter that the one hundred and twenty had in the upper room, on the day of Pentecost with the Holy Spirit, It had my undivided attention. The Bible became a real resource of application because I saw its power and authority immediately. My attention was directly focused toward the Bible and the church because I wanted to know more. When I was baptized with the Holy Spirit I had such a revelation of Jesus and of the Bible. Thinking that this tremendous event which happened to me, also, happened to thousands of others throughout history. I wondered eagerly, "What else had I been missing?" "Why didn't people know about all of these things?" "Why hadn't I heard of such an awesome event during my lifetime?" I was on a major search for truth from that day forward.

It says in the Word that He gives life and life abundantly, in which He surely does. If you are not experiencing the abundant life it's because there is more to tap into. God sent so much for us to receive. It's like an open door or open window at every turn. There is always more! We **all** fall short in recognizing all that God has for us to receive. He is continually waiting for us to seek Him and His kingdom as it truly is. NOT how we perceive it!

> *Matthew 6:33(NKJV) But seek first the kingdom of God and His righteousness, and all these things shall be added to you.*

After receiving Jesus as Savior and then being filled with His promised Holy Spirit, the excitement begins. And to think that's only the beginning. What an entrance into the kingdom. I remember feeling as if I entered a new world. By saturating our self with the Word and communicating with God through prayer, it sets us up for an abundant life. Continually seek Him and listen to Him and it will bring complete fulfillment, which in turn, produces the fruit of the Spirit. I wouldn't live any other way! No matter what comes my way I always know I am never alone and I always know I have someone to talk with that has the answers, I need for my life. People can not fill the place in you that Jesus fills. People come and go and blow with the wind and it is hard to count on even the best of friend or family member, like you can count on Jesus. It is very reassuring to know that *He never changes and His Word never changes.* He will always be there!

> *Hebrews 13:5-6(NKJV) Let your conduct be without covetousness; be content with such things as you have. For He Himself has said, "I will never leave you nor forsake you."*
> *So we may boldly say: "The Lord is my helper; I will not fear. What can man do to me?"*

Yes, I continually see new aspects of who He is and can always go to the source, His Word, and see the same Jesus that so many wrote about in the Bible. Just listen to what people say about Him! Even today I hear the words ringing from those who truly know Him. They proclaim, "He's Wonderful!" "He's a Mighty God, He's Awesome!"

"He's so faithful!" I have grown to love Him because of who He is and how he **relates** to people. There is none to be compared with Him because of his patience, gentleness and great love. In this book you will hear of only one account of someone who has been taught by the very best, Jesus. What He does for one He does for all!

Acts 10:34(NKJV) Then Peter opened his mouth and said: "In truth I perceive that God shows no partiality.

I look back and cringe in fear of the lifestyle I would have today if it hadn't been for His nudging me and wooing me to come join Him in a better life. What a defining moment in time for me and to think I am only a drop in the bucket compared to the millions of people's lives where He has intervened. The Word is just as alive to me as it was twenty three years ago. The only difference is that I understand a little more, have a little more revelation and comprehend to a greater degree who He is and what He is accomplishing right before my very own eyes. He surely has been all I could have asked for and is much more than I could have ever imagined in this relationship. It's been beyond exciting! It's only by His mercy and grace that we get to acquire glimpses now and again of who He is. But whoa…when we get that taste we…

Truly want to see more of Him!

Psalms 34:8(NKJV) Oh, taste and see that the Lord is good; Blessed is the man who trusts in Him!

I know, that throughout eternity, we will continue to learn about the many facets of God. There is an intensity that can be felt about the Lord. Some may not understand how you can have such an intimate relationship with some one you can't see or touch, but remember we can hear Him and feel Him. Unlike many people on this earth, He delights in getting close to you. As you draw near to Him He draws near to you. If I am speaking in a way you don't comprehend I encourage you to STOP everything and turn your heart toward Him and run after Him with all you've got. Don't stop until you are consumed with Him. I am here to tell you that you won't be disappointed but rather will be in for the *time of your life*. He wants to show Himself strong through and to His people.

> ***2 Chronicles 16:9(NKJV)*** *For the eyes of the Lord run to and fro throughout the whole earth, to show Himself strong on behalf of those whose heart is loyal to Him.*

> ***Daniel 11:32(NKJV)*** *Those who do wickedly against the covenant he shall corrupt with flattery; but the people who know their God shall be strong, and carry out great exploits.*

You will hear a great testimony of who He is throughout this book because of many remarkable events that have occurred since 1984. Apparently, He wants me to share my personal relationship and share what and how He has been teaching me throughout these many years. For, by the Spirit, I am compelled to share this personal relationship. He wants you to have a greater understanding of the way He communicates for it has not changed. What you read in the Word He is still doing.

Jesus Christ the same yesterday, and today, and for ever.

That will be my focus in this book. Jesus is assuredly the same Jesus that walked on this earth over two thousand years ago and for some reason that picture has been distorted and somewhat watered down. I believe the church is about to make up for lost time! Over the years, I have found the body holding back (including myself) and I want to encourage us all to enjoy a greater freedom in being who we are as Christians and being free to represent Jesus, accurately. We need a greater release that depicts the true kingdom that has come, as it is in heaven. It is one that is glorious and can be experienced as glorious as long as we stop rejecting the REAL JESUS and His REAL KINGDOM! Break away from the mundane and step over into the miraculous. That is where Jesus remained throughout His ministry on earth, in the miraculous and we are to follow His lead.

I will begin with acknowledging the crucial event that created a major turn in the course of my life that established a much closer walk with the Lord. For those who read my first book, "The Voice of God" *A Church with Hearing Ears,* bear with me as I lay a foundation of what occurred while driving in my car coming home from church one night in 1994. **Ten years** I had been loving, walking and serving the Lord to the best of my ability when I get a huge surprise. I had an encounter with the Holy Spirit that I had never before experienced. I began to hear my prayer language in English. Now to remind you, I had been filled with the Holy Spirit for ten years. I had exercised the gift of speaking in tongues in my private prayer life for hours at a time, ten years, and had never heard English. I had always prayed in my prayer language because it was something I was not going to neglect. If God gave it to me, then I was certainly going to use it as much as I possibly could. Besides, I gained renewed strength in the spiritual sense when I prayed using this God-given language. For ten years I had certainly received wisdom by praying in tongues, but was extremely caught off guard when I began to hear it in distinct English words. At that moment, speaking in tongues had an additional significance. I could understand it. I have always loved using my prayer language and continue to love it as it is a way of communicating with God. Jesus says the baptism in the Holy Spirit is an enduement of power. What a superior way Jesus departed, by sending one to indwell us. What a perfect plan to fulfill His purpose.

Luke 24:49(NKJV) Behold, I send the Promise of My Father upon you; but tarry in the city of Jerusalem until you are endued with power from on high."

*Ephesians 1:13-14(NKJV) In Him you also trusted, after you heard the word of truth, the gospel of your salvation; in whom also, having believed, **you were sealed with the Holy Spirit of promise, who is the guarantee of our inheritance** until the redemption of the purchased possession, to the praise of His glory.*

Right off, as I prayed, I would listen to my tongues and I could hear many different languages coming out of my mouth. To me, it all seemed so miraculous. Even though I didn't fully understand the impact of this language, I could still sense the great importance of it by using it. Paul surely knew the significance of speaking in tongues as he claims to speak in tongues more than others. I too agree with Paul and spend a great amount of time praying in these languages during my private prayer time.

> **1 Corinthians 14:18(NKJV)** *I thank my God I speak with tongues more than you all;*

It surely built me up on my most holy faith. Besides, as I used it, I was glorifying God. What more acceptable and perfect way….God's way! What a God, that He would create something so extraordinary by using the most unruly member of our body and use it for magnifying Him and for the building up of His body.

> **Jude 1:20(NKJV)** *But you, beloved, building yourselves up on your most holy faith, praying in the Holy Spirit,*
> **Acts 10:46(NKJV)** *For they heard them speak with tongues and magnify God. Then Peter answered,*

As Paul himself stated that he spoke with tongues more than most people, we too should follow the example. There is great value in using what God gives us no matter if man places great significance on using it or not. Many are deceived by fads, trends and downright ignorance. We must use what God gives us based on His Word and according to the plain and simple fact that HE IS GOD! His ways are ways that we don't fully comprehend. I have noticed that as we move out of our comfort zones and step out in faith, then, He teaches us things we wouldn't have learned otherwise. If it's in the Bible it can be ours, if we accept it. He gives us the free choice of accepting or rejecting. According to the Bible, there is a lot to accept or reject, starting with accepting or rejecting Jesus as Lord of your life. If for any reason you have not received His Holy Spirit since you believed then begin to ask for this empowerment.

> **Acts 19:2(NKJV)** *he said to them, "Did you receive the Holy Spirit when you believed?" So they said to him, "We have not so much as heard whether there is a Holy Spirit."*

He is faithful in providing all that He teaches us through His Word. Remember, He <u>remains the same</u> to this day. Don't allow

distractions of this world to overshadow the true riches to be had in His kingdom. There are hidden treasures to be found. He has them for us, His people!

Colossians 2:2-3(NKJV) *that their hearts may be encouraged, being knit together in love, and attaining to all riches of the full assurance of understanding, to the knowledge of the mystery of God, both of the Father and of Christ, in whom are hidden all the treasures of wisdom and knowledge.*

Chapter 2
Pray That You May Interpret

The night I was in my car and began to hear my prayer language, started me on a grand adventure that I had not anticipated. I have always enjoyed my relationship with the Lord, but when I began to hear those words in English, I was energized. That night the Lord spoke by His Holy Spirit to me for about forty five minutes. The Holy Spirit began to tell me many things by enabling me to interpret while I spoke in tongues. During the course of that night the Lord commanded me to get with Him two times a week and to write everything down. Little did I know of what He was about to reveal to me. What a delightful time it has been ever since that initial evening. I was in intense training by the Holy Spirit during the first two years. I honestly had to work through a lot of unbelief and lack of discipline. Sometimes it was difficult to stay focused without my attention straying. It's amazing how distracted we can be. Once I realized the impact of what He was teaching me I couldn't get enough. I was running into the secret place continually. In the first year, I filled fourteen journals. Out of those He commanded me to compile stories. There were over 200 pulled directly from the journals. Another year later he commanded me to write a book. He gave me the title, each chapter and what went in each chapter. The book "The Voice of God" A Church With Hearing Ears, was completed in six weeks. Each day, each moment, I spent with Him made me stronger and more in Love with Him.

In the first two years the stories He told me were parabolic and allegorical in nature. I would always begin praying in my prayer language and listen for the English to kick in. It always did and I filled pages as I heard it in English. I hesitated many times as I would sit before the

Lord to begin writing. It just didn't seem possible to be able to hear my tongues in English because I had not heard anyone talk about being able to do this. But each time, when I stepped out in faith, I was blessed and it was incredible as I wrote His words to me. I would see vision after vision as Jesus illustrated all that He spoke. When I began this process of praying in my prayer language and then listening for its interpretation the visions also flourished. I didn't even know to call them visions because they came so natural and I didn't really know anything about visions. I have been very reluctant to share with many people about how I have been receiving revelation for the last fourteen years, until a recent prompting by the Lord to do so. Once I began to operate in this gift, the flow of the Holy Spirit seemed to come very natural.

It's all a matter of seeking Him, focusing on Him and giving Him glory for it all. It amazes me how small a part we actually have to play, which is good. It's good because in and of ourselves there lies very little truth or wisdom that we can impart that does anyone much good. But by His Spirit, we can impart great truths. Wisdom that is inspired by the Holy Spirit is of great value; therefore, we must press in to receive from Him. As I soaked in the Word and continually saw that the interpretations were lining up scripturally, my faith grew. He basically taught me scriptural truths by illustrating and storytelling. As I continued to journal I saw a greater relationship with how Jesus spoke in the Bible and how He was communicating with me. After some time I realized Jesus had particular styles of teaching and speaking. I also had a greater understanding of how the Holy Spirit spoke to people in the Bible. I saw that a man truly could hear specifics, from God, the Father, through His Son Jesus, by the Holy Spirit. He speaks to us and can give us visuals for understanding and clarification. It is **evident throughout** the Word.

Acts 9:10-12(NKJV) Now there was a certain disciple at Damascus named Ananias; and to him the Lord said in a vision, "Ananias." And he said, "Here I am, Lord." So the Lord said to him, "Arise and go to the street called Straight, and inquire at the house of Judas for one called Saul of Tarsus, for behold, he is praying. And in a vision he has seen a man named Ananias coming in and putting his hand on him, so that he might receive his sight."

Yes, there are <u>many ways</u> to hear the voice of God but I am announcing *loudly,* that we can interpret that heavenly language that so many of us have in the world today. All we have to do is ask the Father so that we may interpret it. This is not my idea to go forward and proclaim that the body is missing a blessing, it is His. The Lord began calling me forth to no longer keep this hidden and to encourage the body to pray to interpret. There has always been so much controversy concerning tongues and honestly I didn't want to be a part of it. My experience is that all can receive the language if they are born again and are willing to receive more. Therefore if all received after they believed there could be greater manifestations of His power.

Acts 19:2(NKJV) he said to them, "Did you receive the Holy Spirit when you believed?"So they said to him, "We have not so much as heard whether there is a Holy Spirit."
*Acts 2:4(NKJV) And they were **all** filled with the Holy Spirit and began to speak with other tongues, as the Spirit gave them utterance.*

I have prayed with many people, including all three of my children, and they have all very easily begun speaking in tongues as they were prayed for to be baptized in the Holy Spirit. I have witnessed my mom pray for countless groups of men, women and teenagers. They have all received the Holy Spirit with the evidence of speaking in tongues as they desired it. I have only witnessed four or five people that didn't receive a prayer language and they admitted their fears or reluctance to receive the gift. I know how valuable it is for prayer, communicating with God, and for building yourself up.

Jude 1:20(NKJV) But you, beloved, building yourselves up on your most holy faith, praying in the Holy Spirit,

We should value everything God gives us and want more and more and more because **more** is available! I see how much I lack in my own prayers compared to praying with the Holy Spirit. I see how prayer is much more effective when I pray in the Spirit and then pray with understanding. I feel that the Lord wants us to tap into another way of communication. As we allow the Holy Spirit to speak through us, as we speak in tongues, we gain revelation and understanding. I feel certain that many believers can hear that heavenly language with a great amount of details and specifics. He has shown us many ways that He can communicate to us. He can speak to us in dreams and visions, through our pastors, from our situations and most importantly through the Bible, which names a few. If interpretation of tongues is something Paul tells us to pray for, then, I believe many in the body of Christ can have it and begin to move in that gift freely. His ways are far greater than ours, therefore I urge you to recognize this gift equally as valuable compared to other gifts. I could talk for hours on the benefits of interpreting tongues, but I'm going to make this simple and leave the rest to Him. I think people have not asked for this gift because of the lack of knowledge concerning it. I, as well, did not have understanding or have any teaching on being able to interpret my own tongues.

My only understanding was that there was a gift of "interpretation of tongues" and it occurred in a church body, and it was for interpreting someone else's tongues, as they brought forth a message. Interpreting during a church service can be very powerful in edifying the body of Christ, but, I have enjoyed the availability of exercising this gift with a great amount of frequency in my own home. It has been extremely powerful in my life. Besides, the Holy Spirit is always with me and I don't have to wait for a church service. I don't see the gift of interpreting a message in tongues operating as often as I did ten years ago. It might be more prominent in some churches compared to other churches. This way of interpretation of tongues was revealed by the Lord to me, as I explained in my testimony, and is completely awesome for personal ministry by the Holy Spirit. I rarely hear anyone discuss it as a possibility. Although, since I have been open about talking about it, I have run across several people that have experienced it to varying degrees. Consequently, as you have trusted God in His decision to fill you with His Holy Spirit, I equally urge you to trust God and ask Him for the interpretation of your tongues.

1 Corinthians 14:13-15(NKJV) Therefore let him who speaks in a tongue pray that he may interpret. For if I pray in a tongue, my spirit prays, but my understanding is unfruitful. What is the conclusion then? I will pray with the spirit, and I will also pray with the understanding. I will sing with the spirit, and I will also sing with the understanding.
*1 Corinthians 14:5(NKJV) I wish you all spoke with tongues, but even more that you prophesied; for he who prophesies is greater than he who speaks with tongues, **unless indeed he interprets, that the church may receive edification.***

In this scripture it says that as we pray in an unknown tongue, it can be unfruitful to the ear. Your understanding is unfruitful, not that tongues is unfruitful. But it goes on to say that as we pray in tongues that we can pray in the understanding. This is what happened to me that night in the car and has continued to happen for the last fourteen years. When the Lord showed me how to operate in this gift I was stepping out in faith. But, there it was right in the Word all the time. By praying in tongues during your private prayer time it will produce abundant fruit in your life. Sometimes I have a hard time convincing people to even spend time praying in their God given language. If you have the gift of tongues you must exercise by using this language frequently and not neglect using it. We must exercise every gift from God!

1 Timothy 4:14(NKJV) Do not neglect the gift that is in you, which was given to you by prophecy with the laying on of the hands of the eldership.
1 Timothy 4:15(NKJV) Meditate on these things; give yourself entirely to them, that your progress may be evident to all.

I know there are many people in the body that desire to know what they are saying in their language. Get a **notebook and pen** and pray in your tongues and write what you hear. Wait until you hear English and write it down. As I have said, there are many ways to hear from the Lord and this is **only one**, yet, I feel it is one that has been overlooked or even downplayed. You just don't hear people talk about this. Do you know the number one question I get from people when I explain about the baptism of the Holy Spirit and speaking in tongues? They usually ask, "Do you know what you are saying?" Just last week I was singing in tongues on a family vacation. My brother stopped me and asked, "Do you know what you are saying?" He then proceeded to say, "You are speaking Spanish!" He lives in Miami and recognized it as a real language that he is well familiar with. If the body began to hear specifically what the Holy Spirit was saying in these unknown languages it would be like wildfire. We **all** have a desire to know what we are saying in this language that we have been given and the Bible tells us to ask that **we may interpret**.

So why are we not all seeking for the interpretation? I think it's because of lack of knowledge. I believe the reason people ask if we can understand the language is because it becomes more valuable in the natural mind if we can understand. Not that God is here to appease our logic but I do believe He wants us to understand, to a greater degree, in all spiritual matters, and this is just one way. Myself, I have changed extensively since operating in this gift of Interpretation of Tongues. My learning has become enhanced. My teaching entails greater revelation and I have gained tremendously as a believer, as a wife, as a mother and as a minister. My prayer life has entered a new realm with great discernment and specifics. I have acquired personal wisdom for what God has called me into. I have greater scriptural understanding about so many things in my life because of this journaling in English of what I hear by the interpretation of tongues. My relationship with the Lord has been strengthened beyond belief. My love for the Lord has intensified to where I completely overflow with His love. I feel like…

I know Him instead of knowing of Him.

John 14:21(NKJV) He who has My commandments and keeps them, it is he who loves Me. And he who loves Me will be loved by My Father, and I will love him and manifest Myself to him."

I pray that our walk with the Lord is ever increasing. If you want some **acceleration** seek Him to interpret your tongues. As you hear and have understanding it will cause you to grow rapidly because His Words change us! With a pure heart and clean hands you can come to receive from Him.

Psalms 15:1-2(NKJV) *Lord, who may abide in Your tabernacle?*
Who may dwell in Your holy hill? He who walks uprightly, And works
righteousness, And speaks the truth in his heart;

I will warn that this is not a game or a way to just get your needs
met. This is **His way** to communicate and not **your way** to get what
you want or to get answers you want to hear. You will find out quickly
that the Lord reveals what He wants to reveal and not what you think
you ought to know. There is danger in trying to dictate what we want
to hear. I have learned to be a receptor without any expectations of
my own ambitions. Never forget, He is God and knows what we need
before we ask, or even know what we have need of in our lives. As I
prayed in tongues and heard it in English, I was continually surprised
and amazed at what I wrote line after line. I was also amazed each
time after I journaled. When I went back to read everything He said, I
was significantly enlightened. I will not lead you to believe, that it was
always easy, because I had to shake off unbelief many times. I am also
aware that there were probably things I wrote out of my own spirit too.
Jesus is the only perfect vessel. We are imperfect vessels. I am also one
that does not ever want to fall into error or any type of apostasy. But, the
fruit far outweighed the fear, so I continued in faith. I was very careful
to align myself with His Word (the Bible) and to continue to check my
motives. I also had several people to listen to what I was interpreting
for accountability.

In the last fourteen years I have filled many notebooks. There are
so many testimonies of His GREATNESS that I could definitely fill
several books. My problem is what to leave out. Everything God shows
us is vital. I value every tidbit, every morsel. Just talking about it makes
me hungry to go listen to His voice. I get stirred as I meditate over the
things He has done. Oh, people, He is a great God with a great big heart
for people like you and me. He wants us to understand just as much as
we want to understand. Take that step of faith. He will prove Himself
faithful every time!!

I heard a well known evangelist Oral Roberts say he heard His
prayer language in English on a Christian television show. He said he
waited for it to come back to him. That is where he got many plans
for the ministry and for his building. I don't know the details but I do

know that people just don't talk about this phenomenon. If Jesus has told me to tell people about this, I have great anticipation at what He is about to do. Assuredly, I hate to keep all the blessings to myself in this affluent gifting. I have always thought that, certainly, there is more to this language. What manner of God would deposit His Spirit inside of us and limit the possibilities. Not my God! He is endless with endless possibilities. Just think of the potential if we all began to understand **even some** of that language sent from above. I believe many mysteries are about to unfold in many unique ways by the Holy Spirit. This just might be one of the ways. I am expecting just about anything from the Lord because He has already amazed me beyond anything I could have imagined.

Mark 9:23(NKJV) Jesus said to him, "If you can believe, all things are possible to him who believes."

The Holy Spirit is extraordinary, unique, astonishing, amazing, incredible and miraculous all rolled up into one package sent from above and greater than you or I know! Imagine the possibilities! Imagine the potential. Imagine the impartations! Imagine the PROMISE!

My mind is flooded with the endlessness of us all hearing such specifics. I'm such a simple woman and yet I have attained such wealth in the Spirit by hearing His voice. In the upcoming chapters I will go into more detail about Jesus as a communicator. Many of us don't even know His voice. Yet, His Word says we will.

John 10:4(NKJV) And when he brings out his own sheep, he goes before them; and the sheep follow him, for they know his voice. Yet they will by no means follow a stranger, but will flee from him, for they do not know the voice of strangers.

What must it take for all of us to engage in activities to position ourselves to hear His voice? I saw in a vision as I lay upon my bed praying one night. I saw the hand of God throw gold dust out over the United States. My eye caught many people scattered throughout the United States. Their hands were raised and were positioned to receive as the gold dust fell. But, many places in the United States, there were no people standing with upheld hands ready to receive the revelation. In these places I saw the gold dust (revelation) falling to the ground. It fell and just disappeared. I was disheartened at the sight. Then the Lord spoke to me and said, "Even you have not received like you could." I was saddened and in my heart I knew it was so true. I knew how I had fallen so short of what His true desire was for me. His true desire for us is so vast and hard to envision. I am guilty and repent before Him. I pray that the Lord will help me to be open to receive more because I know that my flesh is weak, but I also know the Spirit is willing. Sometimes I wish I could shake myself to awaken from my own slumber. That's hard to do! Thankfully His mercy endures forever!

Chapter 3
Visions

When I started the journaling I immediately began to have pictorial images as I heard the Holy Spirit. Like I said, I was not really aware of or familiar with the term vision. It took several months to realize that these pictures that I saw were, in actuality, visions. We, as people, are flooded with mental images all of our lives. We don't really think much about them because they are just a part of how God created our brains to work. We picture events, imagine situations and have glimpses of people and things, continually. God uses that same process to show us what He wants us to know. That is why they come very naturally. The difference between the everyday visual image and the Godly vision is that God's vision comes with revelation. They come with an element of surprise. Yes, a person can imagine just about anything in this world but, as you submit yourself to the Lord, He will reveal himself through the vision. With all things that come from the Lord there is also an accountability to them. Where much is given, much is required. Jesus communicates with visions and therefore is a part of who He is and is a part of His kingdom's ways of operation.

Luke 12:48(NKJV) But he who did not know, yet committed things deserving of stripes, shall be beaten with few. For everyone to whom much is given, from him much will be required; and to whom much has been committed, of him they will ask the more.

Keeping a pure heart and a conscious sincerity with the Lord enables you to be a clean vessel in which the Lord will guide his wealth through. We are imperfect beings; therefore we can err quite easily. But as we submit to the Word and submit to the Lord we are able to stay on the right track. This keeps us from getting flaky or envisioning out of our own fleshly desires. It is also very important to submit yourself under the authority of your pastoral leadership. Visions can change your mindset, your focus and give greater insight for your spiritual walk. Visions can also give you discernment and wisdom as you pray. Once you gain maturity God can use you to encourage others by the vision. God has used visions throughout time to change the course of man as He imparts His will in a picture format.

Once we receive Jesus, as our Savior and the Lord of our life, many exciting things can begin to manifest. Remember, He changes us from glory to glory and there are many ways He does this. As we allow the Holy Spirit to move us and convict us, changes will happen. One way change can happen is by the vision. Visions changed the lives of Paul, Mary, Peter, John and changed their course of direction. The actual word or the form of the word vision is used approximately one hundred times in the Bible. They are mentioned countless times in both the new and old testaments. If you are experiencing visions, let people know that they are a part of our Christianity. We must NOT keep quiet about who we are and who Jesus says He is according to His word.

2 Corinthians 3:18(NKJV) But we all, with unveiled face, beholding as in a mirror the glory of the Lord, are being transformed into the same image from glory to glory, just as by the Spirit of the Lord.

A person is transformed by the renewing of the mind, by the Word of God. In today's times the Word can be found in many places and through many avenues. We can be changed by repentance, by reading the Word, by hearing a sermon, by having a dream or seeing a vision. God still speaks to us by the still small voice as He did with Elijah in "1Kings 19:12". The changes and transformations can come any way God chooses. It is awesome how He reveals Himself in so many ways to mankind. I am working on a testimony book and have a testimony of one guy that was alone in his prison cell and in came a ball of light. From that night, and a course of many events, he was never the same and is walking with the Lord to this day because of how God revealed himself. The more testimonies I hear like that, the more it encourages me to pray for the miraculous to occur in the earth today. Maybe we can't be in some of these godless nations or godless places, but guess who can? Jesus can, by His Holy Spirit, and there are absolutely no boundaries. He can surpass our wildest imaginations and do mighty exploits!

One time I was praying and journaling and I kept repeating these numbers in my mind, over and over. I finally wrote them down. I kept praying, but began to look at the number. I noticed it was a phone number. It was a long distance phone number. I finally got up the nerve to call it. When I did, a church secretary answered and told me the church name. I didn't know quite what to say. I boldly came out and told her I was praying for quite some time and that I began to hear this number repeatedly in my head. I asked her if there was something I could pray, for her church. She said, "Oh, wait just a minute, I need to get the pastor." She went to get the pastor and we spoke for quite a few minutes. He was very excited and gave me a few things to pray for him and his church. I told him that I had never had this happen before. Guess what? Years later, I still pray for that church in Weatherford, Texas. I still pray for that pastor and his congregation. You never know what connections God will make, by His Holy Spirit.

At first, when the Lord began showing me these inner visions, He would ask me, "Do you see this?" Then He would proceed to explain some spiritual principal using that object. He was the greatest teacher ever. He began teaching me just like a little child. I have had so much fun listening to Him and seeing His illustrations. The Lord has told me hundreds of stories, illustrating them by vision. He has taken me on adventures by way of vision and taught me through each one of them. As I pray, He illustrates what He wants me to pray. As I minister, He gives me visions and the revelation as I speak into people's lives. When the Lord had me write my last book I saw the title of each chapter in a vision and I wrote them down. I also had the complete understanding of what went in each chapter. In fact, I have seen through the form of visions the titles of several books.

This book, I find, has not been as easy. I had the title and subtitle but wasn't quite sure how to promote its definite message. He is weaning me off of child support by not giving me every single detail. In my experience, the visions from the Lord have often come first, and then came the revelation. Whereas, I think we often naturally think of something first and then we picture it in our minds. Now I'm not a trained professional in such matters, but I consider how my mind works. I believe, because the Lord worked the visions in this reverse fashion, it caused me to be more focused on His Words. I became intrigued by the picture, so I eagerly awaited its meaning. If you see a vision from the Lord you should have the understanding also. To this day if I don't have instant revelation I say to the Lord, "What is that?" or "What does that mean?" Then when the Lord explains I am usually amazed by the revelation of what He is showing me. In many visions the Lord keys me in on a particular aspect of the vision (like a camera lens that closes in on an object). Then He tells me specifics to share or pray. If I don't have revelation I keep it to myself. There is an example of this in the Bible where Peter has a vision then He hears the voice of the Holy Spirit. As you have experiences from the Lord you should see examples of them in the Bible.

Acts 10:19(NKJV) While Peter thought about the vision, the Spirit said to him, "Behold, three men are seeking you.
Acts 10:20(NKJV) Arise therefore, go down and go with them, doubting nothing; for I have sent them."

This next scripture is an encouragement because as He shows us things He is about to perform them. Begin to pray for the vision and then begin to look for them. Remember, they come very naturally and they come with enlightenment. They are repeatedly recorded in the Bible and they can be a big part of us as a body of believers.

Jeremiah 1:11-12(NKJV) Moreover the word of the Lord came to me, saying, "Jeremiah, what do you see?"And I said, "I see a branch of an almond tree."
Then the Lord said to me, "You have seen well, for I am ready to perform My word."

Once I realized that this was very common according to the Bible I relaxed and enjoyed my Savior as He spoke by His Holy Spirit. I learned to accept <u>who He was and how He wanted to communicate.</u> I'm not saying everyone will have visions, like I experience them, because everyone's giftings are diverse. However, you never know how God may gift you unless you ask. I believe visions are available to <u>all Christians</u> at any given time to help in ministry or for prayer. I had been walking with the Lord for ten years when all this additional blessing came my way. Thankfully, I knew the Bible well enough to recognize it was scriptural. But, it wasn't until I began experiencing this more complete relationship did I begin to really search what the Word said about such experiences. I was ecstatic to find that this was what it was supposed to be like. I continually checked the Bible for confirmations on what I was experiencing. I wanted to know that my experiences were lining up scripturally. There it was, proof that this was one of the ways Jesus, by His Holy Spirit, communicated.

If you are not experiencing visions you must begin to ask Him for them. They are very valuable. **All things** given to us from the Lord are of great value. They are for the believer! Check it out for yourself! In James 4:2 it tells us that we don't have certain things because we have not asked Him for them. He also says that He manifests Himself to us because He loves us. If we want to do greater works, as Jesus says we will do, we must do things **His way** and not by our own understanding and in our own way, which always results in dead works.

John 14:21(NKJV) He who has My commandments and keeps them, it is he who loves Me. And he who loves Me will be loved by My Father, and I will love him and manifest Myself to him."

John 14:12-14(NKJV) "Most assuredly, I say to you, he who believes in Me, the works that I do he will do also; and greater works than these he will do, because I go to My Father. And whatever you ask in My name, that I will do, that the Father may be glorified in the Son. If you ask anything in My name, I will do it.

Man places value on so little of what the kingdom has to offer. Jesus told us to ask and seek and that we would not be turned away. We must know there are vast riches to dig up that belong to the body of Christ. Visions are just one way He communicates with us. It is truly amazing how many ways He uses to inform us about things in our midst and of things to come. Visions are readily available to the born again believer. Visions can come for many reasons and are very powerful. They come to teach, warn, to give direction and to reveal truth. They will always draw you closer to Jesus because everything He does draws us *to Him* and draws us *to know Him*. In this passage from the Word, you will see that Jesus also saw what the Father was doing by way of vision.

> ***John 1:48-50(NKJV)*** *Nathanael said to Him, "How do You know me?"Jesus answered and said to him, "Before Philip called you, when you were under the fig tree, I saw you."*
> *Nathanael answered and said to Him, "Rabbi, You are the Son of God! You are the King of Israel!" Jesus answered and said to him, "Because I said to you, 'I saw you under the fig tree,' do you believe? You will see greater things than these."*

This should be an occurrence that happens frequently if we are to SEE what the Father is doing. Jesus says that He doesn't <u>do anything</u> unless He sees His Father doing it. Therefore this should be our ambition. On the next few pages I am going to share particular times when I had a simple inner vision from the Lord. He uses pictures to help us so we will have a better understanding of what He desires to convey. He gives us visions to enhance what He wants us to pray. Peter brought the salvation message to the gentiles because of a vision. Peter had a vision after falling into a trance like state.

> ***Acts 10:10(NKJV)*** *Then he became very hungry and wanted to eat; but while they made ready, he fell into a trance **Acts 10:11(NKJV)** and saw heaven opened and an object like a great sheet bound at the four corners, descending to him and let down to the earth.*

If you read on you will see the mighty illustration that was given to Peter in the Word. What an impact it made on Peter and the Church as we know it today. Of course my revelations seem simple compared to his, yet, I know that our God is not partial to one over another and He will use whoever He desires to impart truth. It is our acknowledgement and our response to what He shows us that is important.

I was on my way to work one morning, and I was praying as usual. On this particular morning I had a vision of this baby being left out in the cold. It was a winter morning and therefore I began to pray fervently about this baby to be found and that someone would get it out of the cold. I prayed other things along this line. I never gave it much thought throughout the day. Being an intercessor, I pray a lot of things and don't have the time to ponder a whole lot on everything I pray. But, as soon as I got home from work my husband was sitting in his chair and being the newsworthy man that he is says, "Did you hear about that baby?" I shouted a bit loud and said, 'What? What happened to the baby?" He then proceeded to tell me about this baby that was left outside and that someone found it that morning. I then shared my story with him. Some visions I have had were never confirmed, like that one. But we must still be faithful and respond to whatever we are privileged to see by the Holy Spirit.

Once I prayed extensively about an African man that was hiding from three white men. I was completely aware that I was seeing into another country because of the surroundings. The Holy Spirit gave me specific information concerning this man according to what I saw in the vision. My prayer was undoubtedly for this man to escape from these men. They were hunting for him and I believe they were going to kill him. I saw him hiding in a barrel of water. I saw him fleeing through the night. I even prayed him into the safety of a couple far off. Now, I could have said, "Oh I am just imagining this!" But when I heard the precise words of prayer coming out of my mouth I knew it was not me. Only the Holy Spirit has the perfect prayers of intercession because He is sent from above. I believe some day I will meet my friend and he will tell me all about the night the Lord kept him safe and gave him the wisdom to find a safe harbor.

Just in recent weeks, I awoke in the middle of the night and had a curiosity about my teenage son. I got up and went down stairs. All the lights were on but he was not anywhere. He is out of high school and I thought maybe he went to his cousins for a visit and had left the lights on. I went upstairs and sat on the couch and just prayed for a moment. I can't even recall what I was praying about. I saw a vision of my son. It was not a very pleasant glimpse of my son and I pushed it out of my mind. It was so graphic that I just tried to dismiss it. The Lord knew this so He showed me another picture of something I had been looking for and then I instantly thought that this item might be in my son's room. God is so Good! Subsequently, I made another trip to the basement to my son's room. While getting the item I heard something that made me investigate. I can not divulge all the details in this incident but, I will say that my son probably would have died that night if it hadn't been for the Lord and His two visions He sent to me. I say this not solely because of my visions, but because my son, after crying and being very upset, told me he also had a vision that night and it was of his death. It was a pivotal point for my son. He had been away from the Lord for a number of years and he had just started turning back to the Lord. The enemy was trying to wipe him out and throw our family off course. But God had other plans. This was a mighty testimony to my son of the love that the Lord has for him. It has also been instrumental in getting his attention. You know what's scary? It is that both of us ignored the visions. The Lord gave us both a vision of the same thing and we both dismissed it. If it hadn't been for the Lord's persistence with me to go back to his room I have great fear of what we would have found the next day.

I was going on a trip to the Bahamas with my husband. I was excited about the trip and was also excited wondering what encounter God might set up while I was gone. So I began praying for His will on this trip. As I sat on my bed I saw a middle aged woman with white hair and a red outfit on. Then the Lord zeroed me in on her shoes. They were red also. Then He even gave me her name. Her name was Evelyn. The Lord told me he would put her beside me on the plane and that all I had to do was to tell her that He loved her and to tell her that I saw her while I was praying. Simple enough! Well, I get to the airport and I am sitting with my husband waiting for our flight. All the while I'm looking for Evelyn. All of a sudden here comes a woman. She has white hair. She is slender. She is wearing a red outfit and most of all she has on RED shoes. Of course, I am a bit restless and I am looking for an opportunity. I get on the plane and guess where she sits? She sits behind me. Now, I know this is no big deal as I look back on this whole situation, but I allowed that tiny detail to completely sidetrack me. I expected her to be beside me (next to me). I stewed and fretted and sadly enough I never spoke to this woman. I was disobedient. To this day it grieves my heart. You know God didn't need me to give her a message, yet He asked me to, and I talked myself out of it. I know somewhere along the line He got His message to her without me. I just feel so grieved that I allowed myself to be sidetracked by that minute detail. Sometimes I think if I had been obedient, I would have walked in greater things sooner. God knows when we are ready for His giftings. Unfortunately, we don't always know ourselves. Visions are important yet I feel many Christians are not acknowledging them. To acknowledge them means to recognize and respond to them. The opposite of **to acknowledge** is to disregard or to pay no attention to. We must value what God gives in His own way of communication. He says His way is not like our way, therefore, we must be sensitive to the way He corresponds with us. We must acknowledge the vision.

John 5:19-20(NKJV) Then Jesus answered and said to them, "Most assuredly, I say to you, the Son can do nothing of Himself, <u>but what He sees the Father do; for whatever He does, the Son also does in like manner</u>. For the Father loves the Son, and shows Him all things that He Himself does; and He will show Him greater works than these, that you may marvel.

Jesus cares so much about us. Even when we think things would be insignificant to the Lord, He shows us that He cares about anything that we are concerned about. Jesus can certainly relate to us because He lived among us as one of us. Just this morning I had the most extraordinary experience concerning a vision. I'm sure many of you will be able to relate to this. Actually, this story began last night. I was looking for a pair of pants that went with this one shirt. I looked EVERYWHERE two times last night. As I woke up this morning, I set out on this mission for looking for these pants again. Except this time, I looked in EVERY place possible at least THREE times. I could not find them. Remembering an incident long ago where the Lord helped me find something, I finally sat down and began like this…. Lord, you give me visions about all kinds of things and I know you know where these pants are. Will you show me where they are? In about two seconds I had a vision. I saw them where they had fallen off the dryer and had fallen between the dryer and the wall. I, excitedly, jumped up and went down stairs to look in that place. I went into the laundry room and reached down along the wall and THERE THEY WERE! Honestly, when I got up stairs, I not only thanked God, but, I cried. I was so touched that He cared enough to reveal where those pants were. I learned something today. If I can ask the Lord where a pair of pants is located and He tells me, then, I can ask about specifics concerning something really important. I can ask about specific areas where people need healing. And I believe He will show me. This vision thing is so very important and the body needs it. It's a part of who we are as believers and it is very powerful. Again, I repeat, it is the way Jesus communicates. It shouldn't be something seen as ooky spooky! IT IS HIS WAY! I tell about this happening years ago, a little bit later on in this book. But, I couldn't resist adding this as I was proofing this book for the publisher on Monday.

I used to be really afraid to tell people about the miraculous things that occurred in my life. For some reason, people don't respond like you think they ought to respond. But, I'm finished with being quiet. I am a firm believer that Christians need to **speak up** much more about visions and dreams, healing, deliverance and anything else Jesus was a part of scripturally. Most people are accustomed to "Jesus Saves". That's Fantastic! <u>What a great beginning, Salvation!</u> Remember, it's not the end! If people were more informed that God gives dreams and visions this world wouldn't be so infatuated with psychic garbage. We have the real thing, yet, we don't always acknowledge the power of Christ within us.

I had dinner with a close friend the other night. She emphatically believes everything died out with the disciples. I'm so glad it didn't! The gospel comes in Word but, it comes in power also. I want the power! Everyone wants power. Jesus, continues today, giving us that empowerment by His word through the Holy Spirit.

Sometimes, we are so entwined into the things of this world that we don't even know who we are as believers. We are in this world but, not of this world. This reminds me of a vision I had during journaling.

In this vision I saw a frog sitting on the ground and instantly his tongue flew out and consumed a butterfly that was passing by. The Lord said, "See how that frog consumed that butterfly?" "This is how the world consumes one that becomes too close to the world."

As we place ourselves before the Lord instead of before the world, He is faithful to position us exactly where we need to be. We want Him to consume us instead of being consumed by the ways of this world. This world does not want much to do with purity and holiness but, God does.

This vision and allegory helped me to see how the positioning is very important. What our hands are on will be the guide in where we are going. We need to keep the pace and be diligent. There is a place for all things and God has it all planned out. Balance is key!

See the bike? There is a place to put your hands, a place to put your feet and a place to sit. See the position? There is a place for all things to be in order according to God. Your hands guide your body for whatever you put your hands to, I will bless. Your feet will take you from place to place. If your foot slips your pace will be lost. The place where you sit brings the balance to the whole thing. You need balance.

We need to be in the right position for God to use us. We need to take hold of what God has for us. He sent Jesus to begin a new covenant. We needed a mediator and a friend. We need to keep up the pace with The Holy Spirit. He has much to show us and teach us. Often, we waste too much time. Thankfully, He is always faithful.

I was in church one night and the Holy Spirit took me to the picture show once again. The Spirit began speaking as the vision unfolded. **Run to grab a piece of the Rock!**

There was this great crater in the Earth and many people surrounded it and gazed upon it. They wondered what had caused this great thing. Then, they turned to one another and asked emphatically, "What has caused this?" And all of a sudden a man arose out of their midst and said loudly and sternly, "This is THAT which God has thrown to the Earth and has **impacted** the Earth!" Then all the people rejoiced and were very happy. Then all the people ran into the crater and grabbed a piece of ROCK and took it out to the world to share what they had heard.

This is a perfect illustration of what we must do. We have to share Jesus, the Rock. He has many facets and if we don't tell people ALL about Him then who will? He has impacted the earth greatly in MANY ways. Don't sell His message short. It starts at the cross, and it continues in a wide variety of ways and activities. We don't want to miss any part of His example during His time on earth. Powerfully so, we have the extension of the Holy Spirit's continued work as Jesus is seated at the right hand of the Father.

He has given us the Holy Spirit and as we are sensitive to Him, greater insight will be given in this dark world. In this vision, I see God's people like an owl. God gives us special abilities to see in the darkness just like the owl. Listen to what the Spirit teaches.

I have sent the Spirit to reveal, to all, the things to come. Have you ever heard of an owl hooting at night? So shall this thing happen (in the body). Just as the owl hoots at night he also sees in the night. He knows everything that is around him, even though others can't see at all. Why? Because I have given him eyes to see. Where one might grope in the darkness, I have given the owl the sight to see. (Then I saw the owl's head turn all the way around) I have given him the extension to see. I have given the owl wisdom to do as he is called. Only, the unwise, do not do what they are called to do.

Just like the owl, we have been created to do certain things. They come as natural as with the owl seeing in the night. Sometimes I think we only tell people certain aspects about Jesus. Just read the Bible, it's loaded with the miraculous and it is a complete picture of who HE is. I know when I mention dreams of the Lord or if I dare mention anything about a vision, among some Christians I, sometimes, get funny looks. It shouldn't be like that. I know we have to be wise in sharing with others but I look forward to being able to share more freely. Some Christians don't believe in laying hands on the sick or believe that Jesus heals today, one of the simplest of truths, "That Jesus Heals". Some times I want to say out loud

"Will the real Jesus stand up! The problem is that it's not any problem with Jesus. The problem is with US!

Acts 14:3(NKJV) *Therefore they stayed there a long time, speaking boldly in the Lord, who was bearing witness to the word of His grace, granting signs and wonders to be done by their hands.*

I am getting ready to go to a publisher, for the first time, to publish three books. A few days ago, I was reading an interesting and powerful book and right in the middle of reading I feel impressed to pray for my first book "The Voice of God". I stopped and prayed many things, seemingly, inspired by the Holy Spirit. Then, out of the blue, I have a vision. I see the oval office. Then, I see the President's desk. On his desk I see my book. I didn't think anything about it until I stopped praying and picked my book up again. When I picked it up I began reading where I left off. This is what I read.

Matthew 10:18(NKJV) *You will be brought before governors and kings for My sake, as a testimony to them and to the Gentiles.*

As soon as I read it I thought WOW! Then I read on…. It said…. What do you say when God gives you an audience with a president? Oh my goodness! Now, I'm really impressed! I eagerly stop again and prayed according to the vision that I had just had about the book and the oval office. I almost always pray according to what I see. I really sort of dismissed this vision until it followed with some confirmation. Will the President every read this book? I'm assuming he will. My faith in what is revealed is strong. Will it bother me if this vision is not confirmed with a final confirmation? No, not at all! I have to walk by faith and not by sight. I respond to what is given. If I'm wrong, who cares? If I'm right, I prayed in obedience. It is all so amazing to me and I want in on it ALL!

That Bible defines Christ, His kingdom and the body of believers. We are joint heirs and are partakers in all His riches in glory. If we seek Him and His righteousness He will add many things to us as believers. Let's don't miss out on ONE thing!

Romans 8:16(NKJV) *The Spirit Himself bears witness with our spirit that we are children of God, 17and if children, then heirs heirs of God and joint heirs with Christ, if indeed we suffer with Him, that we may also be glorified together.*

One time I was praying in the Spirit and all of a sudden I saw myself looking over a hole. I looked into the hole and yelled, "Jesus, are you in there?" Again I yelled, "Jesus, are you in there?" The next thing, I found myself **IN** the hole. It was dark and dank and it didn't look like it was going to be so easy to get out. I looked all around and said, "Lord, are

You in here?" I looked upward and knew I was stuck. The Lord spoke to me and told me to be careful not to go into things when I didn't know for sure if He was in them. He said that I could find myself in a place I couldn't get out of.

Those kinds of simplistic visuals made and make a great impact on my life. I never want to live without hearing and seeing things from the Lord. My life seems so enriched and full, compared to days gone by without the Lord.

Matthew 4:4(NKJV) *But He answered and said, "It is written, 'Man shall not live by bread alone, but by every word that proceeds from the mouth of God.'"*

One of my first visions occurred when I was a fairly new Christian. I had been looking for something diligently for three days and whatever it was, I needed it. I finally plopped down on the sofa and bowed my head (you have to bow your head ☺). I said, "Lord I'm not getting off this couch until you show me where that ____ is." Instantly I saw the thing in the corner of this box. I went straight to that box and there it was. I was amazed and began teaching my children to ask God to help them find things. Guess what? He did just that! He helped them on many occasions. Just as I said earlier, He cares about those little things just as much as the big things because He cares for us. In later years my son was looking for something and couldn't find it. It struck me to ask him, "Did you pray and ask the Lord where it was?" My son later confessed that he scoffed at first, but then went ahead and asked the Lord where this item was. As soon as he prayed, he immediately saw the item under the bathroom sink. He ran out with the item and told me his testimony. It was a testimony reminding him whose son he really was.

Just the other day my nineteen year old son looked for quite some time for his cell phone. I caught him searching under the couch cushions. Moments later he came upstairs with a big grin on his face. He said no one can help him like HIM. He told me that he had stopped and prayed and turned around and there it was. He remembered those days as a child.

I love the Lord's Words. I love what He shows me. I'm such a simple person and love His simplicity. One time I was praying for this couple.

I saw a bird, a Toucan. I told them I saw a Toucan and the Lord says, "You Two Can!" They were overjoyed with laughter because they knew that it was from the Lord. They were leaving and moving to Florida and were going into ministry. It was such a simple vision with such a simple message. Yet, it was a great encouragement. That's God!

If you think God is showing you things, begin to acknowledge them by responding to them. Do not dismiss them. Continue to seek God in the midst of them. He never disappoints the seeker. My number one question to God is, "What is it Lord?" This is a very easy gesture. We don't mind asking people this question. Sometimes I have complete revelation, but sometimes He wants me to communicate with Him more concerning what He is showing. He wants us all to get in position to receive from Him. He wants us all to converse with Him on a regular basis. I use many visions as a basis for prayer. I see things, then I begin to pray and it begins to grow into revelatory and prophetic intercession.

At times, the Lord gives visions so that I will perform prophetic acts. I was going to a concert to pray at the entrance of a local concert hall. This person coming to give a concert is a well known singer. He is well known for perversion in his concerts. Days before I went, as I was praying, I saw myself spit into a water bottle. Immediately I rejected it. I even thought, "I am not doing that!" Then I inquired of the Lord. Then the Lord showed me himself as He added spit in the dust "John 9:6" and then He said that He had spit in the dirt and placed it upon the eyes of the blind man so that he might see. He said He wanted me to spit in the water bottle containing water and squirt it along the doorways so that as the people went over the threshold into the concert that they might see and recognize the perversion. They would have eyes to see the truth about this man and his displays and no longer be blind to the truth. As soon as He said that, I agreed with great enthusiasm.

Sometimes we just need a little more understanding to walk in faith and He is willing to do just that. Like many believers I want to have a balance as I go about doing things and just want something in scripture to validate it. Jesus understands that and is so willing to confirm His Word to us. In fact, it is good to have confirmation. It is not good to <u>always</u> make it a requirement because we must come to a level of faith and of maturity. The confirmation may not always come so quickly either. I do know God wants His people to be obedient and to be faithful in trusting Him. Sometimes it takes us moving forward and we don't have to have thunder and lightening to prove it's from God. Remember we are created by Him and His ways come very natural as long as we don't harden our hearts or stiffen our necks to His will. We would never think of holding our own child's hand, continually after he has learned to walk. The Lord wants us to eventually move with more freedom also.

1 Corinthians 13:11(NKJV) When I was a child, I spoke as a child, I understood as a child, I thought as a child; but when I became a man, I put away childish things.

Hebrews 11:6(NKJV) But without faith it is impossible to please Him, for he who comes to God must believe that He is, and that He is a rewarder of those who diligently seek Him.

I think it always comes back to our heart and He knows if you come to Him with sincerity or not. He knows your motive to having insight and will pour out treasures to the one that sincerely desires more of Him. We must come with a pure heart and pure motives. His giftings do not come to make **us** look good. They are to glorify God! Pride can be a reason for our disobedience. We can be centered on ourselves by only caring what we will look like if we fail. **He knows** when we don't step out in obedience and **He knows** exactly why we don't. He's looking for people He can trust and is looking for people that are obedient. He's looking for a remnant that fulfills the purposes of God and has the heart of God in mind. Is this you?

Here is a vision that is a perfect illustration of how we can be at times. We have to grow up and not always expect earthly rewards for what we do. Our reward is in heaven and there is nothing unseen by the Father. Either it will be pure enough to remain as a reward in heaven or it will be burned up and counted as a waste.

Feeding Flesh

I saw a seal. I saw that it did a task and then I saw someone throw it a fish for doing the task.

The Lord said, "Don't always expect something for each task." "It only feeds the flesh."

I love the process of transformation. In nature, it is miraculous. As God transforms us it is also miraculous. As we are patient He always completes the work He begins.

Transformation

(I saw a tadpole and the many changes it goes through)

Egg-Tadpole-Loses tail-Gains legs. The Lord focused me in on how it walked. It went from swimming to hopping.

Then the Lord said, "Now people are like this, when they are born again. They learn to swim. Then I begin to add and take away one thing at a time. Then I teach them how to climb out of water and really cover ground in a new way."

Remember, we are all in a process of being refined and changed. He molds us and shapes us according to our purpose in life. What get's crazy sometimes is that we are all in different areas of that process.

Process

See the ice cubes? See how they drop out and have been fully formed? There was a process to this. First, there was a filling up. Then there was a process of forming by transformation. A change had to be made. Then the finished product came out and the purpose was fulfilled.

(ice cubes to cool my drink-Ha Ha)

The Lord has continued to show me every day items to teach me. He did the same while He was on earth over two thousand years ago. He is the same yesterday, today and for ever.

Philippians 1:6(NKJV) *being confident of this very thing, that He who has begun a good work in you will complete it until the day of Jesus Christ;*

The Lord showed me how in the body of Christ that we must be patient as He works in other people's lives. Sometimes we can be impatient and often times intolerant of others. God is not finished with any of us. We may be doing real well one day then oops.... something will pop up and shows us how short we fall!

Here is a vision of two loaves of bread in the oven. Then the Lord began to speak by His Spirit.

Ah, I see that one has fallen and has not risen like the other. What happened? Both went into the oven and both received the same amount of heat. (firey trial)

(Then I see someone shake the one loaf of bread!)

Oh, one has been shaken! This has caused it to fall.

So while one is in the process of the fire and is shaken, it can cause a fall. Who has done this shaking? It is one that is unknowledgeable of the process of the fire. This is the body of Christ that does this.

The Lord showed me how delicate of a situation this can be for those that are in the midst of a trial. We must encourage each other and not cause each other to fall.

We all have purpose and God deals with each of us individually. Only He can bring us into the kingdom through salvation, prepare us, and then get us to our destination. We are one, yet, we are individuals with a wide variety of callings. Have you found your pocket yet?

Alignment

I saw pool balls being racked symbolizing people that were being brought into alignment. They were being readied for dispersion and then being cued by the Lord to be put into various pockets for service.

My final vision is a message from the Lord to take our walk with Him seriously. We can have so much fun with Him but it is a serious matter to serve Him with excellence. As we are patient with one another and align ourselves with Him we will be able to overcome any obstacle. We do have to stay close to Him. It's always a safe place. When we run off, problems occur. He has taught me so many things. He is here to teach us all. He is a great one to revolutionize me and you. What a blessing!

Take It Seriously

(I saw a little boy walking down a pathway)

He began skipping and didn't take His walk seriously. Then he fell and scraped his knee. He got up and a tear ran from his eye. He said, "Why has this happened to me Lord? The Lord reached His hand down to the boy and said, "You did not take your walk with me seriously, therefore you got hurt." "Take your walk seriously."

Visions have been an obvious benefit to being a child of the King throughout the Bible. They have been a tool that the Lord has used to teach me for many years. He has warned me about things and has given me greater understanding about things. He taught me countless truths for me to live by. I believe visions are ours in the body of Christ. He gives giftings severally as He wills. (1Cor.12:11) Begin to ask Him to communicate to you by way of vision.

As I was reading Isaiah 29:10-11, it talks about the vision being sealed. So, by the prompting of the Holy Spirit I pray that the vision be unsealed for the body of Christ! If it can be sealed... it can be unsealed! Lord, unseal the vision for all who read this, that multitudes may run with the vision. So Be It!

Chapter 4
Parables

Jesus is the same communicator today that He was when He was on the Earth. This book is being written because Jesus has revealed Himself as being the same person as He has always been. After all these years of listening to the Lord and listening during my journaling I finally have a better understanding of His style. I knew He was talking to me like He talked to people in the Bible but, I didn't know enough to put my finger on what manner in which He spoke. Jesus is the greatest teacher there ever was because of His style. He could get people's attention because of how He spoke and what He spoke. His teachings were so profound and full of truths that people still use them today. Over two thousand years and people are still quoting Him because of the power of His words. I would assume that most people know that Jesus spoke quite often in parables and used analogies throughout the new testament of the Bible. He gives many analogies and tells many allegories as He teaches. If a person wanted to understand Him more they could actually go into great study just solely on how Jesus communicated through the scriptures. There are many books, to my surprise, on the subject. I am not a biblical scholar, just a person who met Jesus and then began digging to find out more about Him.

My testimony is ever increasing because of His continued communication by His Holy Spirit. It seems that all my experiences with the Lord come, and then I am able to support them from seeking them out and finding them in scripture. He has always kept me in the Word of God seeking out truth. I was completely unaware that Jesus by His Holy Spirit would clearly communicate with us, even though the Word tells us He will. Sometimes I think He has had freedom with me because I don't know a whole lot. Let's just simply say, my mind doesn't get in the way of what He wants to do. I don't say this sarcastically but with much laughter. So often I have been clueless!! I don't even have any ambitions, of my own, for these books. But, I know How He works and He has a purpose for all things so I put my hope in Him. I know in my own self I can't make much happen. It's like I fall upon what He gives me, to my great delight! I'm just trying to listen to what He is telling me to do and then I have to leave the rest to Him. That's hard enough for me to do without having any attachments or requirements on things. It seems that He puts the cart before the horse in my life and I always have to run and get the horse. I run to the Word because it is the driving force to all revelation. Revelation is carried by the Word of God. That is what makes it powerful.

I can't tell you how many times I was reading parts of the scriptures and it reminded me of a story the Lord told me. Frankly, I have not been a fast learner. I am still on a mission of trying to figure out what Jesus is doing. He never ceases to amaze me. Even when I have all the writings in books right in front of me, I am still clueless to what He is getting ready to use it all for. The treasures can be right under our nose and until He is ready to shed light on it or bring revelation, it remains a mystery. It's like, after I filled my first fourteen journals, He had me go back and mark the stories. There were over two hundred stories and words of wisdom that I typed up from those journals. I was flabbergasted! I am, again, at that same place. I have gone through the many journals to date and am still not knowing what He is about to do. I just go forward in what He says to do.

I love this time with Him. I stay passionate over the call of God on my life solely because of His ingenuity, faithfulness and the love that He places in that call. What love I have experienced! I am sold out to Him. I truly delight in what He is doing, even when I'm not really sure what it is all about or even know the full impact of what He is doing. I honestly thought we were <u>just having fun together and INDEED we were!</u> However, I limit God in my own plans. I can say I wholeheartedly trust Him in what He plans. Now that I said that, I suppose a test will come!

I knew I saw direct similarities of the Lord's style by comparing the words in my journaling to the scriptures. But, it wasn't until recently that

I understood the greater relationship of the two. There is a correlation because of the manner in which Jesus speaks. In the days when the Bible was written, Jesus was seen as a spectacular teacher. People flocked to Him just to listen to Him. Of course, He backed His words with power as He performed the miraculous. His style of speaking is the same, whether it's from long ago or whether it is to us today. He has been a mighty story teller during my private time with Him. It is evident to me that He is still living and communicating just as He did over two thousand years ago. I certainly do not put my journaled words at or above the scriptures, so, please do not **misunderstand** me. I do value them as Words being spoken by the Holy Spirit from Jesus to me, as a child of God. Whether anyone else values them or even believes that Jesus still speaks today is not my task in this book, nor do I want it to be. His Word stands alone and sets up His statutes. It will be your choice whether to believe He still speaks or not. The longer I am in relationship with Jesus I see that He does want people to know Him as a communicator and that He wants to communicate with us just as much as He did when He was on Earth, except now He communicates by His Spirit which He sent on the day of Pentecost. This is a twist for some in a day like today. The Word truly has to renew our minds to come in alignment with His ways of doing things.

John 14:16-18(NKJV) And I will pray the Father, and He will give you another Helper, that He may abide with you forever— the Spirit of truth, whom the world cannot receive, because it neither sees Him nor knows Him; but you know Him, for He dwells with you and will be in you. I will not leave you orphans; I will come to you.

Jesus made this promise to us, before He left this Earth. He wanted us to know that He was sending another one to enable Himself to communicate with us and vice versa. In my mind, all of the things that He spoke to me were mine alone unless instructed otherwise. Knowing that I'm sharing my whole relationship puts me in a vulnerable position. I was completely happy where I was. Now the Lord pushes me out of my comfort zone. Nevertheless, He has done it all, therefore, I submit it all!

Parables are stories that illustrate a spiritual truth using earthly things. These things are similar, yet, different. Jesus told over fifty of these types of stories in the New Testament. He used everyday items, plant life, animals, and people as illustrations in His stories.

Matthew 13:9-13(NKJV) He who has ears to hear, let him hear!"
And the disciples came and said to Him, "Why do You speak to them in parables?"
He answered and said to them, "Because it has been given to you to know the mysteries of the kingdom of heaven, but to them it has not been given. For whoever has, to him more will be given, and he will have abundance; but whoever does not have, even what he has will be taken away from him. Therefore I speak to them in parables, because seeing they do not see, and hearing they do not hear, nor do they understand.

Jesus intrigued many by using parables. They were like riddles to be solved with profound meaning of His kingdom. They interested the people because he used common things of that day, to explain a **kingdom they were not familiar** with at that time. He only revealed the meaning of the parables to those that had ears to hear. Storytelling commands an audience and He mastered that as He taught the masses. In the past fourteen years He has also captured my attention as He has told me story after story. I would hang onto every word as I hurriedly wrote them down. I found that He told me many truths pertaining to His people. I became aware of the Lord's concern over people because He seemed to tell me many stories which pertained to us and our walk with Him. I began to have a true heart for the body of Christ only because He did. Here is a modern day parable given to me that describes our journey with the Lord giving us a kingdom focus.

The Journeyman

A journeyman set out on a course. As he set out, he prepared all that he had need of for his great journey. He packed many supplies for the road that he intended on traveling, which was quite long. He carried along some tools. He took a hatchet and took a shovel for he planned much work along his travels. He grabbed his hat and left all behind to take out on this great journey. As he left, many saw him off. They stated,

"Farewell good man and may it be well on your travels." The first thing he encountered on his journey was an enormous rock. It was right in the middle of the road and caused this hindrance to him moving on. He called many men to come and help remove this great rock but their efforts were quite futile. Just as they would lift the rock, it would fall back into its original place. In spite of all effort to move the rock, the task was impossible. The man stopped and thought for a very long while. He pondered the situation and came up with a great idea. He thought that if he could break up the rock, he and others could remove the rock in pieces. He told others of his plan. They agreed, with such a marvelous plan. So, then they began to carry out the plan to remove the obstacle. Bit by bit, piece by piece they removed every part of the rock. "Well done!" they encouraged one another. They had accomplished the job at hand and accomplished it to completion. Now for the journeyman, his travels had just begun. He grabbed all his supplies and carried on. As he began down the road, he looked back and thought on the situation at hand. He felt an inner peace for the job had been completed. While his mind pondered on things of the past, also, things were soon approaching his path. The next encounter on his road was a stream of trees running clear across the road. He looked at them and saw their perfect and strategic placing. He took out his hatchet and began to chop at the base of the first tree. Chop, Chop, Chop went his hatchet. Down it went! Then the next tree, then another. One by one the trees were laid flat and provided a clearing once again, on the road.

The Lord said You will see that on this road, that I have you travel, shall be many obstacles. Although the obstacles may be great and may be many, there shall be a way prepared for the <u>Way of The Lord.</u> Much teamwork will be needed and much effort shall be used to prepare this way. But, thus Saith the Lord, I shall give you all that you need to accomplish the task and I will supply you with all the wisdom to do so.

For this is what I have each of you do, Prepare the Way of The Lord!

The one main message in this parable is to prepare the way of the Lord. We do this as we are unified. When we see our brothers and sisters in Christ struggling we have to come together in one bond and remove obstacles to prepare that way. The enemy will try to stop us from doing what we are supposed to do, but, no weapon will be formed against us that will prosper.

Luke 3:4-6(NKJV) *as it is written in the book of the words of Isaiah the prophet, saying: "The voice of one crying in the wilderness: 'Prepare the way of the Lord; Make His paths straight. Every valley shall be filled And every mountain and hill brought low; The crooked places shall be made straight And the rough ways smooth; And all flesh shall see the salvation of God.'"*

It really amazed me how often the Lord spoke about His people. I got a real good idea, quickly, on where His focus was. My love increased for the body because of His love. My prayers were greatly increased for the body of Christ. As you search out the scriptures over half of His parables, in the Bible, involve people. He loves people and therefore cares about all things concerning people. He wants us to know about His kingdom in a way we can understand because His ways are not like our ways. In Matthew 13 beginning with the 34th verse it describes a time where the disciples inquire about the parable of the wheat and the tares. He is willing to divulge its significance and its meaning. As He explains it thoroughly they begin to understand. He then begins a series of analogies of His kingdom.

An analogy is a comparison or correlation of one thing to another. It might have similar likenesses or resemble it in a particular aspect. The analogy in Matt.13:44 describes His kingdom as being a hidden treasure. Oh my! He is so fascinating how He delivers His messages. In Matthew 13:54 the people are astonished and amazed at Jesus' wisdom. I too have felt that about Him as I sat time after time listening to all of His wonderful words. He will speak to you today just as He has spoken to those of yesterday. And guess what? He will speak to us, our children, and our children's children. He has established a covenant with us. We must respond to Him! He is waiting for all of us to come into this wonderful fellowship. He walked in the cool of the day with Adam and Eve. He spoke face to face with Moses. He spoke to Paul in a vision and Solomon by a dream. He spoke to many by His precious Holy Spirit, long ago, and is still speaking to us by the Spirit today. Guess what? He will speak to us for ever by His Holy Spirit until the day we go on to be with Him. That tells me how much he desires to be with us. It's awesome!

John 14:26(NKJV) *But the Helper, the Holy Spirit, whom the Father will send in My name, He will teach you all things, and bring to your remembrance all things that I said to you.*

An allegory may have hidden meaning or symbolism.

Here is an allegory about His people. I sensed His delight as He spoke this to me.

The Latter Rain

Do you hear the rain? The Latter rain? It's refreshing! All of my beautiful flowers need this latter rain. The seeds need this latter rain. You will see all the things grow. It will be in full bloom. Then an angel of God will come and pick all the fully bloomed flowers. They will be ready for the banquet table.

The latter rain is the last outpouring before His return. The seeds are what He has planted in the Earth concerning His kingdom. The fully bloomed flowers are those people ready. The banquet table is where we will sit for the marriage supper of the Lamb of God. We are going to be the beautiful bouquet of flowers for the Lord.

Some parables and allegorical stories are prophetic and foretell of things coming. The next story is one given to me many years ago. Listen to this illustration of His coming. Remember, as I have said, the Lord gives me visual pictures as He speaks. This one was thrilling as I saw this story unfold.

The Fire In The Forest

Listen to the excitement!
Listen to the people!
He's Coming Soon!

It's like the fire in the forest. The closer it gets the animals run in a heightened excitement. They know their surrounding and know there is a change, a change that is coming. With the animals the fire is an unknown source, but with my people Jesus is not an unknown source.

You know of His coming because He forewarns. He bought you for a price. He'll not mislead! As the fire gets closer, also in the hearts of my people I will create an increase of burning. There will be a frenzy of activity from the enemy also. Many will try to put out the fire but will be unable.

This is a fire that can not be quenched!

You should have seen those animals running around. What an illustration of intense excitement in the kingdom. I think there is that excitement today for His soon return. Whenever I talk to people that are walking closely with the Lord they comment that they are all sensing an intensity that something is about to happen. I don't know exactly what is about to take place, but, I assure you I feel it too. Here is another story about a fisherman.

The Fisherman

There was a worn out old fisherman. He was very old. He looked a ripe age of 80. He continued to be faithful in his fishing. Year after year he carried his rod and his tackle. Now, he was out one day at dusk. The lightening struck the water and gave him a great fright. All of a sudden the fish began to float to the top, one by one. He ran around and scooped them up and put them on the small amount of ice. That night when he went home he carried a large amount of fish to his wife. The old woman looked in surprise. She said, "Such an old man to catch so many fish." He said, "I carried on as usual and then, all of a sudden, there was a loud sound as a clap of thunder!" "Then all around me was the catch of all catches, too numerous to bring home." "So this is the story of my day."

But, I say as the Lord of all, "There will come a day that my voice will call out and the "catch of the day" will be quite numerous, for I will call many to the surface."

In this story the fisherman symbolizes someone, maybe, that has been in the ministry a long time being faithful to the great commission. The great commission means bringing people to the knowledge of Christ. The thunder is God's voice. The wife symbolizes the Church witnessing a great incoming of salvations like she's never seen before. The lesson taught is about the coming harvest during the end times. The

Lord presents Himself in the thunder and lightening in the parable and also in this scripture. His power is greater than we can imagine.

Exodus 19:16(NKJV) Then it came to pass on the third day, in the morning, that there were thunderings and lightnings, and a thick cloud on the mountain; and the sound of the trumpet was very loud, so that all the people who were in the camp trembled.

The parables of Jesus are of great variety. The parable about the speck in one's eye teaches us about judging others. In Matthew 13, the parable of the mustard seed teaches us how His kingdom grows. Jesus' parable about the two debtors teaches us about forgiveness. Also, the parable of the ten virgins warns us to be ready for His coming. Jesus has given us many ways to understand and to receive His message. We must have ears to hear what the Spirit is saying to the Church because we are the Church. Not only must we search our hearts as we read His Word, the Bible, we must also hear for ourselves what He is saying to us for this hour, for our own lives. Get quiet before the Lord and be ready to listen. In my first book I am quite emphatic about why you must hear His voice. It is so vital that we hear Him. He longs to communicate with us each day. He is willing and available. Access has been made because of His death on the cross. According to the book of Hebrews we are able to enter boldly to the throne of grace. Jesus made a way to enable all who receive Him to receive guidance, direction and teaching from His Holy Spirit. Once we receive Him we must go back and tell others. Here is a story that brings tears to my eyes because of the truth it imparts.

You Must Go Back To Tell Them

There was this little boy. He was lost from his mother. So, he went up to many people and said, "Do you know where my mother went?" Of course their answer was no, for they did not even know his mother. He dropped his head and said, "No one knows my mother and therefore does not even know where I can find her." Then the little boy looked up and there, all of a sudden, was his mother. He ran up to her. Then he ran back to all the people and said, "See, this is my mother!" "See what she looks like?" "Isn't she nice?" Then the Lord said…This is like you. When you are seeking me you might ask others of me. But, when you find Me you must go back and show them Me! You must go back and tell them of Me!

Jesus teaches us so that we may live His abundant life right here on this Earth. He tells us things so we will grab hold of our inheritance as believers. Sometimes, for various reasons, we stray in our beliefs. Sometimes we try to make things happen. It takes Jesus to keep us focused. Here is a funny little story that puts things in perspective.

A Fish Out of Water

There once was a fish. He would swim, but delighted in seeing the birds above. He would gaze at them and delight in there flight. He longed to know what it was like to fly. He pondered on ways that he too, could fly. He thought, "Now if I could swim so fast I could go from the water and enter the air." But then he thought long and hard. He thought that maybe there would be danger entering the air in this manner. So, he thought again. Once more he came up with a good idea. He said, "Now if I could just flip myself up out of the water, maybe God would give me wings and then I would fly." Again he thought and figured this was not the will of God.

Then the Lord said… For I say, stay where you are, doing what I have created you to do. Do not come up with ways to maneuver yourself into things not designed for you. For I have a plan for each of you. My plan is perfect. My plan is a plan of all plans. I shall tell you of things you should enter. Do not be like a fish out of water for you shall surely die.

There have been many stories that bring admonishment or correction to me and the body of Christ.

Zechariah 4:6(NKJV) So he answered and said to me: "This is the word of the Lord to Zerubbabel: 'Not by might nor by power, but by My Spirit,' Says the Lord of hosts.

Here is a story about how we try so hard to get God to move. Sometimes we think we can control God. We act as foolish as these fleas!

It's By My Spirit

There were these fleas. They were jumping on a trampoline. They did not even create a bounce in the trampoline. For what movement they created was of their own. (Their bouncing up and down) They spent many hours doing this only to realize that their efforts were futile in trying to get the trampoline to move.

I say, this is so like My people. They put tremendous effort into the movement of My Spirit. But, I say that this is not of me. I have not said, move. They move on their own accord. They go without Me. Now for all those fleas, they still go back and try to get that trampoline to move. But I say, until I send you, don't go.

The Lord commands us to assemble together with other believers for good reason. Here is a story that gives a good reason to listen to His words of wisdom.

Don't Be Separated

See this piece of straw? It came from a large bail of straw. Someone pulled it out from the rest. What was the purpose for this? (I saw a person chewing on a piece of straw)

One might want to chew on this straw. One might want to remove it to break it into pieces. One might pull this piece of straw out only to examine it. For all these reasons, the enemy might have for removing you from the body of Christ. Forsake not yourself from one another.

*Hebrews 10:23-25(NKJV) Let us hold fast the confession of our hope without wavering, for He who promised is faithful. And let us consider one another in order to stir up love and good works, **not forsaking the assembling of ourselves together**, as is the manner of some, but exhorting one another, and so much the more as you see the Day approaching.*

The enemy wants us to separate ourselves from the body. We must remain in fellowship because we encourage one another and bring strength to one another. The enemy wants to break us! God desires that we be in unity. If we separate our selves from believers we are isolated from His purpose in using us as a complete entity. The Lord wants us together so that we might provide that dwelling place for Him as it talks about in the book of Ephesians. He is fitly joining us together and desires that we be holy as He is holy.

Here is a story that completely caught me off guard with its ending. He has amazed me at his story telling.

Holiness

A washtub! A woman may wash her clothing on the scrub board. (I saw an old time scrubbing board) She scrubs and she scrubs. Oh, finally she spies a hole in the article of clothing. Afterward, she determines that this article of clothing is worn out. It's been cleaned and cleaned. Finally, it comes to the end of the line of its use. But, I say that my people are not like this. I clean and I clean and see there are no holes. But when I clean there is righteousness. When I clean a holiness comes. YES, YES, see there is a holiness that comes. This holiness is not because of its worn out state but because it is being prepared for its further use.

This makes me realize even more how His ways are not like our ways. How does He do that? I'm still amazed!

I loved the stories the Lord told me that were humorous and simultaneously held a specific truth. In this story, I see a little candle. This little candle was so cute. It's a shame it didn't recognize its source! Some times we look past all the ways the Lord tries to rescue us. Have you ever done this?

When Your Flicker is Gone

(I saw a little candle)

There was this little light. It flickered day and night and then it went out. It looked around and saw darkness. It strained to be lit again. It jumped up and down to create the light it once was. It just wasn't there. Then, all of a sudden, there came a knock at the door. It walked over and opened the door from which the knock came. When it opened the door there stood a stranger. The stranger said, "How are you?" The light said, "Well I'm having trouble." The stranger said, "Well, how can I help?" The light said, "You can't help, there is nothing you can do." So, the stranger went away. Then came another knock at the door. This knock was a long, slow knock. The light decided not to answer this time.

Then the Lord said...

I have been calling you and you have not come to the door of opportunity. I have been knocking and you have not answered. I have sent others and you will not receive from them.

Many stories of the Lord have been extremely humorous. The vision was just as humorous. I have laughed so hard as I listened and watched. As I wrote, sometimes, I could barely keep from laughing myself off the couch. Jesus is funny. We are made in His image. Where do you think we got our sense of humor? It is from Him! I'll never forget when the Lord showed me this clown. Most of all, I'll never forget the message that went with it.

Missing the Mark

(I saw this clown putting on his makeup. Every time he tried to put the red lipstick on and around his lips the tube of lipstick would slip and run up the clown's face or down the clown's face and neck.) It had me in stitches.

There was this clown. He was putting on his makeup. As he was trying to put the makeup upon his lips he kept missing. His makeup slid up his face and then it slid down his neck.

I heard the Lord laugh and say, "It really isn't this bad!"

Now the clown was very frustrated and wondered why he kept missing his mark. He tried very hard and each time he would miss his mark. This is so like My people. Do you want to know why? My people keep trying to hit their mark. I say, they never will. It is comical for them to think they will. But, I will take their hand and with My guidance they will truly go the right way. They are going to miss their mark many times but with me, they will have the right makeup!

I had a friend that passed away several years ago. This next story was one of Connie's favorites. I'll share it with you in honor of her.

Just A Little Bit Of Jelly

(I saw this clump of dried up jelly lying on a counter top)

There was just a little bit of jelly. It lay upon the counter. It blamed the spoon for its mishap. As it lay there blaming the spoon, it began to dry up. It became hard and not supple as it had been created. Then along came a dishrag and gave it relief. As the dishrag smoothed over the jelly it once again was supple. It arose out of its hardened state and rejoiced for the dishrag had brought it back to life again.

So it is like unto My people. I shall smooth over them the moisture that is needed and once again they shall be renewed. They shall be sweet like unto jelly. But most of all, they shall be lifted.

Many times in our lives we blame others and oftentimes become bitter over situations, but with Jesus help our heart are softened.

Psalms 3:3(NKJV) *But You, O Lord, are a shield for me, My glory and the One who lifts up my head.*

This next story and vision was one of the most powerful and truly majestic. It made me want to leave immediately to be with Him! It was so vivid and I could hear that loud screech piercing the atmosphere. It was a mighty call! And the anticipation of the birds was intense.

His Flock Will Meet Him In The Air

There was this great bird. He was bestowed with much strength and was a very powerful bird. He swooped down out of the sky with greatness. He passed many on his flight. Many gazed at him with an expectancy. They waited for him to notice them for when he saw them, he would do great things. He would land on tall mountains. He would fly with a swiftness that no other bird could fly. But, unlike other birds, he had a screech that **all** would hear.

(I then heard a loud bird screech that was awesomely powerful)

When he screeched, all upon the ground heard. When they heard him they joined him in the sky. They then knew they were his! They knew that they were a part of him and were on the same flight with him. When they met him in the sky they then knew that **they too** possessed the same power that this great bird possessed. They too soared to great heights. They too knew that they belonged to this flock!! They went to great heights with this great bird. He took them to places they had never been and had never seen. He amazed them with the things that he showed them.

So, I tell you that these days that you stand and watch the works of the Lord, you too will be a part of these great things that He has created.

(Then I had the most awesome awareness that the things he had to show us after we are taken from this world would be beyond our wildest imaginations)

I am looking forward to these things that He will show us. While the Lord was speaking I saw the whole scenario in vision. It was something! Those smaller birds upon the ground watched in such amazement. The smaller birds symbolized us, His body. I will never forget that loud sound, that screech, of the powerful bird (Christ Himself!). The Lord is so awesomely powerful. I can only vaguely imagine what He has in store for us. I think of the scripture that says that the Holy Spirit is just a deposit of what is to come.

1 Corinthians 2:9-10(NKJV) But as it is written: "Eye has not seen, nor ear heard, Nor have entered into the heart of man The things which God has prepared for those who love Him." But God has revealed them to us through His Spirit. For the Spirit searches all things, yes, the deep things of God.

In many of the stories that the Lord would tell me, by His Spirit, He would show me what He was going to do in the body of Christ. He would also let me know what He saw as areas that needed work in the body. This story is one of my all time favorites. As I spoke in tongues, while journaling in 1995, I heard and saw this vision. This illustration set me on a mission to pray for the body of Christ for many years.

The Body

It's alive! It's alive and well on planet earth. It causes turmoil. It causes much trouble. It is a spirit that runs rampant upon the earth. It is a spirit of confusion. It must be bound. Bind confusion in the body of Christ.

The hand thinks it's supposed to slap the face. The foot thinks it's supposed to kick up dirt. The nose thinks it's supposed to smell for trouble. These things are all wrong. All the body parts are in the wrong place, doing all the wrong things. (Then I saw a human body and all the body parts fly off into all directions)

Then the Lord proceeded to say. I am going to take each part and talk to them. When I send them back to the body they will begin doing their proper job. They will have new insight and new direction.

The hands will come together and work together. The feet will walk in unison. The ears will listen together and the mouths will take turns to speak. The eyes will watch together. They will keep track of all the other working parts. The heads will organize. They will join together with ideas that I have planted within. The knees will join together in prayer and intercession. The elbows will join together and produce much work. The hearts will hear the voice of God and pump the messages to the rest of the body. I will then lay the body down and give her dreams. I will provide healing in every part of the body. When she rises up she will feel good. She will feel organized. She will feel unified. She will be in one mind and one accord. She then will walk upright and holy. She then will walk the path of righteousness. She will then grab the people by the wayside and they will join her. The people by the wayside will desire to walk in unity with her because of Me.

1 Corinthians 14:33(NKJV) *For God is not the author of confusion but of peace, as in all the churches of the saints.*
Corinthians 12:12(NKJV) For as the body is one and has many members, but all the members of that one body, being many, are one body, so also is Christ.

I believe this story has been fulfilled except for the ending. I believe there is a mighty wave of healing coming to the body. I also believe, along with many, that we are on the verge of a Great Awakening. There will be a **great outpouring** of Salvations that will be at the center of this revival with great multitudes coming into the Kingdom of God. I believe the body is in her finest hour. We must wake up fully to what God is doing.

Dream-The Bride

In the mid eighties I saw, in a dream, the bride of Christ. I saw a woman in a bridal gown lying at the foot of a garbage heap sound asleep. There was a bulldozer coming in and removing all the garbage. Then I saw the Lord's huge hands scoop her up. As He did this she slowly woke up and yawned. As she was stretching and yawning I noticed she had dirt smudges on her face and on her wedding gown. Then I saw the Lord begin to clean the smudges off of her. Then I woke up. This dream caused me to begin to pray for the bride of Christ. I still pray for Him to wake us up and clean us up!

> ***Ephesians 5:25-27(NKJV)*** *Husbands, love your wives, just as Christ also loved the church and gave Himself for her, that He might sanctify and cleanse her with the washing of water by the word, that He might present her to Himself a glorious church, not having spot or wrinkle or any such thing, but that she should be holy and without blemish.*

Chapter 5
Dreams

Godly dreams can be quite impressive. A dream occurs while one is asleep and will get the undivided attention of anyone who has one of these types of encounters with God. Dreams were used to communicate God's will in the Old and in the New Testament of the Bible. The word depicting a dream or night vision is used approximately one hundred times in the entire Bible. This phenomenon was a frequent experience according to scriptures. Dreams can serve as a teaching, a warning, for giving direction or revealing truth. God gave people dreams thousands of years ago enabling them to receive a message from God. There are over thirty dreams recorded throughout the Bible and are depicted from Genesis to revelations. They occurred for a variety of reasons and God still continues to give us dreams today.

Jesus Christ the same yesterday, and to day, and for ever.

God spoke, in a dream, to Jacob in Genesis 31:10, giving him wisdom about choosing his flock according to their markings which caused him to become a rich man. Joseph prophetically dreamed dreams of his future which angered his brothers to the point that they sold him into slavery. Joseph was also one who could interpret dreams, which created a turn of events, thereby placing him in a position of great authority. Solomon was given a gift of great wisdom through a dream. Joseph and Mary were given dreams which gave them direction and in turn brought about safety for themselves and Jesus. Dreams, like visions, are another part of our make up as humans. This therefore makes it another natural process for God to use for communication. Dreams from God are very distinct and should not be confused with the ordinary dream. A person usually recognizes that there is something special about a dream from God. It's possible not to have the interpretation of a dream from God but He will give you understanding as you seek him. Various tenses of the word dream over one hundred times. Dreams were a very common form of communication to man by God. Typically, when I have a dream from the Lord it is very specific and is usually very detailed. Most often, I awaken immediately after the dream and then God will speak something to me or I have a strong impression of something. Several times, the Lord brought confirmation the next day concerning the dream. Be careful not to label words, dreams or visions as from the Lord unless you have a confidence in knowing they are from Him. We don't want to misrepresent Him in any way. Yet, we still want to step out in faith and share what the Lord is giving us. There is balance in all things and we can help each other and encourage one another as we hear from the Lord.

I read once that Thomas Edison dreamed about the light bulb and therefore invented it. I read that Abraham Lincoln dreamed about slavery being abolished and also dreamed about his own death. If a person were to investigate into dreams they would possibly find many people throughout history having significant dreams that changed their lives and probably changed our lives too. Unlike visions, where I feel you can put yourself in position to receive more, dreams can not be controlled. At least I have never seen where I could get them to occur more frequently. Just all of a sudden, without warning, they occur. I do believe that as you ask God to give you dreams He will be faithful.

Matthew 7:7-8(NKJV) *"Ask, and it will be given to you; seek, and you will find; knock, and it will be opened to you. For everyone who asks receives, and he who seeks finds, and to him who knocks it will be opened.*

I have had God dreams from the beginning of my walk with the Lord. They were infrequent but they occurred to create powerful images that I still envision today. They still positively affect my life as I walk with the Lord. I think the dream is very realistic and is not easily forgotten. My first dreams as a new believer were to teach me the "Power of the Name of Jesus". The first God dream I had was one where Jesus taught me authority using His name. In the dream I was dreaming I was asleep. Up over my mattress came long fingernails, clawing at me, while I was sleeping. It was apparently the devil's hands and they were trying to get me. I was a brand new Christian. In my dream I fearfully, frightfully and very timidly spoke, "In the Name of Jesus." I immediately woke up from the terrible nightmare! Yeah! God wins! He began teaching me immediately, kingdom strategies. That was my first type of God dream and several more were to follow. I found myself being robbed and ridding the robbers by commanding them in the "Name of Jesus", to leave! I saw snakes being run over by cars as I shouted, "In the Name of Jesus!" The snakes would rise back up and I would shout again, "In the Name of Jesus!" Again the snakes would be run over by cars and flattened. I also heard demons in a basement shriek and shrill as I shouted out, "In the Name of Jesus!!!" They fell back and withdrew because of **His Name**! Those were my first teachings by Jesus in dreams. I think He wanted me to know my authority over the enemy as soon as possible!

There didn't seem to be any rhyme or reason in my mind for when a dream occurred except that it was His will for it to occur. You would think He would give you a dream because you have reached a place in your life of greater spirituality, but I have not found that to always be so. Remember Joseph? He bragged about seeing his brothers bowing down to him. They didn't take that so lightly. In my immaturity, I had one of the most exciting dreams I have ever had. When I was first married, I was mad at my husband, shamefully I was taking the alternate place to sleep, the couch! Unexpectedly and undeserving… here it comes, **the dream**.

In my dream I was standing at the edge of a vast sea and it was at night. There were two glowing pillars, one on each side of me. I proceeded to walk out into the sea about waist deep. As I stood there I felt the most glorious presence of the Lord. It was as if waves of increasing glory swept over me. With each wave it intensified. I have felt his presence and surely it is wonderful, but, this was nothing I had ever experienced before. At last, when the feeling didn't seem like it could get any better I turned around and there sitting on a smaller stone pillar was Jesus. He was wearing a white robe and the whole place seemed to have an iridescent bright look. I could not see any facial features and Jesus' head was just a head shaped light. I saw ticker taped words running across His forehead and on His robe. I was straining to read all the words. I remember reading Lord of Lords and King of Kings. Then I woke up. At the time, the message was that I was struggling with reading His Word. It made me press into His Word. I think also that Jesus just wants to reveal himself to us. I remembered feeling saddened because the first time I saw Jesus I was out on the couch, mad at my husband. Do you think He did that on purpose? Anyway, I ran in and woke my husband up quietly and told him I saw Jesus in a dream. The "wow factor" has always been in place from the very beginning, for me, with the Lord. The more He revealed to me the more I wanted!

Because of the dream I now knew the power of His Name and knew the power of His presence. The dream has been profoundly impressive and I wish I had more of them. It's only been in the past three to four years that I have had another stream of God dreams. Some of them are prophetic. Of course, sometimes, a dream will have later significance because they are prophetic. In Gen.37:5 Joseph had a prophetic dream, as a young boy, of his brothers bowing to him which later came to pass. This happened to my son as his revelation came ten years later resulting from his prophetic dream as a child.

My son had a dream when he was around nine years old. He dreamed he was looking everywhere for this ring that Jesus had given him. In the dream, he looked and looked and finally he found it. But, when he found it, it was broken. He walked up to Jesus and handed it to Him. As Jesus took the ring he closed His hand and then he handed it right back to my son. When Jesus handed him the ring it was fixed and was no longer broken.

My son thought that was so cool and has never forgotten that dream. Well, I never really knew either what it meant until just recently. My son is nineteen and has been away from the Lord and has just recently started coming back to the Lord. A few months ago while we were at church our pastor began preaching about Jesus and how he has given us a ring. He preached that because we have broken covenant with Jesus. He kept saying that we had lost the ring. My son and I looked quickly at each other with wide eyes. Our pastor went to some length talking about broken covenant which was another milestone to bringing my son back to the Lord. That sermon was directly intended for my son and was exact in its message. The Lord knew ten years ago that my son was going to backslide and walk away from Him. He knew my son was going to come back to Him after breaking his covenant with the Lord. The Lord cared enough that He gave him a dream many years ago just so He could communicate to Phillip that He was going to fix it. What a powerful testimony to my son of Jesus' love for Him. What a testimony to me as it touches my heart, as a mother. That dream gave me increased faith knowing that God is in control and that He cares about all things!

I have had some recent dreams which I know are prophetic. They depict a time that is futuristic in nature. One night I had a dream where I died. I was escorted to hundreds of rooms which were depicting my life. The time seemed to never end and I could hear music everywhere I was escorted. I only remember a handful of the rooms. Some were of good things and others had aspects of things I needed to do. One room that I went into had all these children sitting and they were shaking my hand and thanking me. (I have taught elementary children for many years)

One room served as a reminder. It contained a big book on a podium. It was a Bible and it reminded me to read the Word. As I was escorted to each room the door would open and it was brightly lit. After going to what seemed like hundreds of rooms I was escorted down several corridors. Just as I was going down one corridor I found myself perpendicular to another corridor. As I was passing that corridor I caught sight of Jesus just coming around the corner. I craned my neck to get a longer look at Him. He was wearing a deep dark red robe and He had a stern look on His face. He was being escorted by several men on both sides of Him. The next thing I know is that I am standing in front of two very large double doors. They swing open. I stand at the threshold and see an arena of thousands of people. They are conversing with one another in a cheerful manner and it appeared to be a very active place. I see off to the right an area of bright light but can not see what is happening. It is the area for which all those people are there for and it seems to be where the main event is occurring, even though I can not see off that far. I then have a strong desire to step over the threshold and enter in, but as I take the step, I wake up. I hear the words, "Great White Throne of Judgment!"

Revelation 20:11-12(NKJV) *Then I saw a great white throne and Him who sat on it, from whose face the earth and the heaven fled away. And there was found no place for them. And I saw the dead, small and great, standing before God, and books were opened. And another book was opened, which is the Book of Life. And the dead were judged according to their works, by the things which were written in the books.*

In that dream, it taught me that someday we will be accountable for everything we do while we are here on earth. I believe we will see our whole life, just as I did in the dream. Jesus was serious about the coming judgment and we had better be in the right place so we will hear, "Well Done good and faithful servant".

Dreams serve as warnings. Joseph and Mary fled with Jesus for safety to Egypt because of a dream. The wisemen were directed to go another route because Herod sought to harm them. So, they were warned in a dream. I had a couple of warnings by way of dreams. They were very short dreams but to the point. They were warning me to not be distracted in my van while I was driving.

Once, in a dream, I saw a snake and leaned out of my car to pick it up and I plummeted over a ravine. This happened again in another dream. As I was leaning over in my van grabbing something on the floorboard I went straight over a bluff. I took these two dreams very seriously and continue to fight distractions while driving in my van. Some time later, after telling my youngest daughter about the dreams, we were in the car. Apparently I was getting distracted while coming down the knobs in which we live. She smacked me on the arm and yelled, "Mommy, remember the snake!" She had remembered the dream and reminded me quickly. If we are willing to follow His directives He is there to keep us informed. Jesus wants us to be aware of things that can bring unnecessary harm. He wants to intervene, but, we must be willing to listen and adhere to His warnings. I hate to say this, but even when we know God has sent a warning we continue fluttering about being careless in our ways. I thank Him for His mercy.

Matthew 2:12(NKJV) ***Then, being divinely warned in a dream that they should not return to Herod, they departed for their own country another way.***

I have recently had a dream about both of my children which I can not divulge. But, I will say it was very specific and was warning both of my teenagers. I typed it up, explained what it meant and left it in their hands. They responded to it and I believe it will serve as a reminder for their fragile lives. Already key points of the dream have been continual teaching points as I have been there to guide them through certain situations. Once we have a dream from the Lord we must respond to it. If it's a dream to teach, learn. If it's a dream to warn, take action. If it's a dream of revelation, impart it. We must respond to Godly dreams in some way. God is looking for a response. We tell our children not to go in the street for a reason. We expect them to follow our directions for perfectly good reasons. We are God's children and He communicates in many different ways for direction in our lives. We just don't **acknowledge** it often enough to achieve total victory. It may be a feeling to do something or it might be a message from the Pastor on a Sunday morning. Our heart might be sparked as we are reading the Bible. It might be sparked through a vision or a dream. We need to be acknowledging all that God communicates in whatever manner He chooses. This is KEY.

Philemon 1:6(NKJV) *that the sharing of your faith may become effective by the acknowledgment of every good thing which is in you in Christ Jesus.*

Bear in mind, acknowledge means to *recognize it, respond to it and react to it.* The more we listen, the more we put ourselves in position for God to communicate to us. You know what it's like, for those with a grown child to have to back off from giving advice. After a while, if your grown child just does whatever he/she wants, you just raise your hands and let it go. In a sense God does this too, yet, all the while He works behind the scene on our behalf. I would much rather have Him right out front working on the scene so I can see His glory, acknowledge His presence, recognize His intervention and submit to His ways. This reminds me of one of my friend's favorite scripture of the thoughts God has toward us.

Jeremiah 29:11(NKJV) *For I know the thoughts that I think toward you, says the Lord, thoughts of peace and not of evil, to give you a future and a hope.*

It was miraculous how Jesus communicated, by a dream to my son, His concern for my son. He communicated, to the extent, that He would go to such lengths for him. His thoughts are good toward us and bring about positive change. Of course it is nothing for the Lord to intervene and reveal Himself in this manner, to prepare us for Him. But, it is EVERYTHING to us. It's a testimony how the Lord works in each of our lives from the day we are born. The Lord has always shown people how much He cares. He still overwhelmingly intervenes for us, encourages us, comforts us and motivates us. As we lend our lives over to Him fully, He will show Himself strong and faithful every step of the way. We must have eyes to see and ears to hear. We must acknowledge Him in all of our ways.

Jesus communicates to anyone He chooses by dreams, including children. I have seen this on occasion with my own children. He wants to teach them about whom He is and what His Kingdom is about. My daughter had a very interesting dream when she was very small. I have never forgotten it. In her dream, Jesus revealed salvation's process. The dream began with a woman holding a baby in her arms. She was going down a creek jumping from one stone to another. There were people on both sides of the creek. They were cheering and clapping their hands, "Come on, you can do it!" Upon hearing this, the woman would leap to yet another rock getting her farther down through the creek. The people all continued to cheer her on when all of a sudden the woman stepped upon a set of steps and went through the doors of a church. That is a perfect story of how the body of Christ encourages people to receive the Greatest gift of all, Salvation through Jesus. It takes the whole body to do this.

I have had several evangelistic dreams where I am leading groups of people to the Lord. They are very exciting, But none as exciting as a dream that I had last year. I dreamed I was in a place and I was attending a huge Bible study in a cafeteria. When I pack up my belongings and begin to exit the meeting I hear a commotion across the room. A friend of mine is standing and yelling across the room. Two men are trying to get her to sit down and to be quiet. They are taking their hands and are pressing her back. She continues to yell and anxiously point at me from across the room. She emphatically yells, "I need to talk to Shirley Hall!" "I need to talk to Shirley Hall about God!"

The next scene I find myself in a room where I am awaiting this friend to talk to her about God. As I walk over to the window I see the most horrific storm I've ever seen. There are the blackest clouds and the most turbulence I have ever seen in a sky. As she arrives I look at her and say, "There is no place to hide!" After that we then began to search for some place to get shelter from the storm. There didn't seem to be anywhere to go to get away from it. Then I woke up. I was certain this was a dream from the Lord and I felt an expectancy that the Lord was about to do something. That morning when I arrived at this particular place I see this person. Laughingly I say, "Boy, I had a dream about you last night." She responded with something funny for she is a very humorous person. Later that day we end up sitting beside each other during a break. She turns to me and says, "So, tell me about this dream!" I just respectfully told her I wouldn't be able to right then, but that she might want to stop by later on and I would tell her about the dream. The next morning I see her again. She eagerly remarks that she wants to hear about the dream and that she will be down at our next break time. As she arrived I told her the dream. I didn't really know exactly what to say so I questioned her if she really did want to know about God. After that, she broke down and told me that something had been bothering her and that she had been talking to her friends about something that had just happened. She seemed amazed at the coincidence. She confided that the other day she was in the kitchen with her son. She made some sort of comment about God. The look in her son's face told her he didn't have a clue what she was talking about. She had a sudden realization that she had gone to church when she was younger, but her son didn't have a clue about anything concerning God. She had not taught him anything about God and it had extremely saddened her, creating brokenness in her heart. In the end she received Christ and I prayed for her for a few other things according to the dream. God orchestrated the entire event. It was His desire to touch her and therefore, used a dream. I give Him all the glory!

The power of dreams can be life changing. We are being transformed by the renewing of our minds, by the Word of God. His Word can come in the form of a dream today! Be ready to value God's dreams. Be ready to record them. Be ready to respond to them. In addition, be ready to impart the wisdom from them.

Last year I had two dreams. One was about the coming of the Lion of Judah. Revelation 5:5 describes His coming. Matthew 25:1 tells about ten virgins. Will you be ready when He comes?

Lion of Judah

I was in a house and was aware that the house had spiritual people in it, along with me. I looked in the front room and saw three girls sitting on a couch laughing, talking and cutting up. I walked into the living room to find a man and a women sitting on the couch. I assumed they were a married couple. Being Christians, I began to introduce myself and told them a small bit of my testimony when I got saved. The woman jumped up and began to tell me how this man had been touched by the power of God some time back. At that time the man got up and walked over to me and took my left hand. Immediately, I felt a surge of power that convinced me that God had surely touched him. A strong power ran up my arm to the elbow. At this time, I was on the floor thinking about how my whole arm was tingling with this surge of power. Then a thought came to me. I kept thinking and quietly stating,

"Unless it be to the Glory of God...it's for nothing". I stated this about three times.

The next scene I was asleep, lying on my back, on a couch in a back room of this same house. I was so sound asleep when a little boy came right over the top of me and within inches of my face he said loudly, "Come and See!" I was so groggy and saw him in clouded vision. I mistakenly said, "Ok Nathaniel" Again he repeated loudly, "Come and See!" I quickly corrected myself as I awoke. (I heard emphatically from within, "This is not Nathaniel...This is David!") I said sleepily, "OH, OK David" and I got up to go with him. He took me outside and it was at night.

David pointed up to the sky and said, "Look!" I looked up and all the stars had gathered together and formed a lion's head. David said,

"Look, It's the Lion of Judah and he is coming!" As he pointed to the right of the stars he said, "The saints are on His right." Then pointing to the left side of the Lion's head formed from the stars, David said, "And the righteous are by His side." I then thought in amazement, "This is an awesome sight to see!" At that time, two girls were coming out of the house talking and laughing and just being social as the girls on the inside had been. I yelled to them and said, "Look up there!" They, nonchalantly, looked up and then with no response walked on their way.

I awoke!

I woke up promptly and knew immediately by the Spirit of God that the girls were the five foolish virgins. I also knew that the boy was King David as a child awakening me to the knowledge of Jesus' second coming. He is the Lion of Judah. The three girls in the house plus the two girls outside just laughing and goofing off symbolized the five foolish virgins. I understood that the man that touched me, presumably by the power of God, was not necessarily of God or either he was not giving the glory to God for the miraculous.

Here is another dream I had several months later. It is about the Jewish people and a planned holocaust. All I can say is that both dreams have caused me to pray for the body of Christ and for the Jewish people. I have also shared with a few intercessors concerning these two dreams. I may not have the complete understanding of them but I've tried to respond to them the best I know how.

Praying For Israel

I was with my natural family in the United States and we were searching for a place to live. We were looking for a place to hide and live. Something had occurred, to place us in this position. We were in a car pulling a camper with our belongings when our camper got stuck.

The next scene I am in a completely different setting (not America) with dirt and cobblestones as the streets. It resembled a town in the Middle East and could very well be Israel. I am an older Jewish woman with a scarf around my head. I am walking through a street with shops. I am trying to hide my identity as being Jewish. I am looking for a place I can hide my family, to live. I have a lengthy scarf draping over my head and I am even trying to, somewhat, hide my face. As I look up, on occasion, I catch the eyes of three different men. They are also Jewish and they are doing the same as I am. They are looking for some place to hide, some place to live unnoticed. I know them and they know me, that we are Jewish. No one else seems to know our identity. I walk into a shop and instead of being a shop it is a small museum. It is a museum of the past atrocities of the Holocaust. I see pictures and small items of torture from the previous holocaust (under Hitler). I notice that it is minimizing the horrific holocaust of the 1940s. I walk and continue to look around and then go down the street and enter a very large factory that looks like it is under construction. I spy a hole in the concrete, way in the back in an uninhabited part of the factory and I think about it as a place of refuge for my family. I continue to travel this enormous factory. I go to another floor and I see in a very large room, two Jewish children, being fitted for these uniforms and fitted for shoes. They had everything taken from them and they were going to outfit them in these other items. There was a very large stack of uniforms and these special shoes that they were making for the Jews. In the dream I was under the impression that there was a plan to repeat the holocaust except this was going to be on a much larger scale. It seemed to be on a grand scale after looking around and seeing the various artifacts being prepared in this factory. I went to another floor and saw a gigantic area of a place where they were baking bread. There was bread everywhere. The bread was in the ovens, on shelves and on huge trays. It looked as if the day was done for the baking of the bread for there were no people around. The bread was sitting and cooling. All of a sudden, off to the back, I spy the very same holes in the construction that led to the place I had thought I could bring my family to hide. My next thought was, "And look at all this bread!" "This is what we could eat."

Then I woke up.

I knew this was a dream from the Lord.

I wondered all morning, "What was it, exactly, that God was trying to tell me?" Then I thought maybe I needed to pray about the Jewish people and about another holocaust being planned against them.

A few hours later, I flip on television and I see John Hagee and he is sitting with a Jewish man having a conversation. They were discussing a possible coming holocaust against God's people and Israel. He is also telling about his new book, "Jerusalem Countdown". To say the least,

I went out and bought the book and began to pray. I gathered with my closest friends, most of which are intercessors in the body of Christ. We had an interesting meeting and prayed for Israel and the Jewish people.

Again, I am not sure of all the details in this dream but I feel that it is a prophetic dream. I ask you, also, to pray for the Jewish people. Many events are occurring in the world today that point to difficult times ahead. Even we in the United States could be headed for times of trials and tribulation. Please pray!

I will share one last dream. It is definitely a prophetic dream. It was incredible and by far the most thought provoking of any dream I have ever had.

Is it Time?

It was night and I was standing among some trees gazing up through an opening and was peering into the sky. As I gazed up into the open area of a starry sky I knew it was a familiar place and it was a place I had gone before. As soon as I thought this, I knew I was about to go there again.

I raised both hands together towards that area of open sky. As soon as I did this….I shot towards that area of open sky at an incredible speed, at an alarming distance! All at once I halted in this position before the SUN. I knew it was the Lord and I had an awesome awareness of where I was, before the Son/sun. I was in AWE!

I shouted loudly…

"IS IT TIME?"

The sun moved as if to answer me. The sun increased in size and closeness 3 times in GREAT POWER! Then the sun reformed into what looked like images of itself, like reflected light of itself. The sun was in the middle but four other images were surrounding it.

Then, I was thrown back to Earth at an incredible speed and landed in a sitting position on the ground outdoors. Where-in I noticed a pile of cut up words that were a bit scattered upon my arrival. I then gathered the cut up words and looked for a place to put the words together. I looked around for my bedroom to do this job. I woke up.

After the dream, I saw a vision of my journal and found it, surprisingly, in a side table. I recorded the dream, immediately. I know that all those cut up words represented the writing and recording of the dream, itself. I believe it is time for the Lord's return. My position, with my hands uplifted, represented an hour hand. I still am not sure about the three movements of the sun. I know it's significant! I know He was answering me with "Yes, It is Time!"

When the sun reflected itself, into the four other areas, I felt like it represented the four corners of the earth. My thought was that He was going to touch the four corners of the earth. My immediate thought, in the dream, when I was ascending through the atmosphere at that incredible speed was that it was the Rapture. Isn't that interesting?

Dreams are assuredly the way God communicated long ago and He has never changed. He still gives dreams **today**. Are you having any God Dreams? He gave dreams to people in the Old Testament of the Bible. He gave dreams to people in the New Testament of the Bible. He gives dreams to people all across the world. Pray that He will give you dreams. Pray that He will give people all across this globe, saved and unsaved alike, dreams that will change their lives. Pray, additionally, that you will act in response to the dreams according to His purpose. As He communicates by way of dreams we must have a reaction. It should bring about change in your life. Dreams have made profound changes in my life. They have been instrumental to my spiritual growth and have given me direction in my walk with the Lord. They give me a source in which to pray, and teach me many things.

Acts 2:17-19(NKJV) *'And it shall come to pass in the last days, says God, That I will pour out of My Spirit on all flesh; Your sons and your daughters shall prophesy, Your young men shall see **visions**, Your old men shall dream **dreams**. And on My menservants and on My maidservants I will pour out My Spirit in those days; And they shall prophesy. I will show wonders in heaven above And signs in the earth beneath: Blood and fire and vapor of smoke.*

GET READY!

Chapter 6
God of Wisdom

As I read the Bible I hear great wisdom. God has communicated wonderful messages to us. The Bible, from beginning to end, is one big guide for us spiritually and for us in our natural lives. His words are life and produce life. When God sent His Son He sent Himself in earthly form. As Jesus walked on this earth He amazed people by His words and by the way He taught. I too have been amazed at the words I have heard as I journaled. It seems that Jesus could minister to one or two or to one thousand and be happy in either situation. He is humorous in what He says and throws people off guard continually by His wisdom. I have learned so much over the past fourteen years by listening to Him, by His Spirit, and have filled forty six journals. I can't say everything I write in my journals is God alone because as long as I have an earthly body I will err. I am completely aware of this. All I can say is that Jesus, by His Holy Spirit, began this work in me and I shall never return to the old way. It has been the most exciting life thus far because of His communicating with me. I have immensely enjoyed this two way relationship. If I never heard His voice again I think I would die of a broken heart. That is what His Words have meant to me.

Throughout my times with the Lord He has given me little tidbits of wisdom. They are like proverbs and I love them. Sometimes I don't completely understand all the things I hear and I am okay with that. I have understood enough to know that Jesus is who He says He is. I have understood enough that I know He's going to do what He says He's going to do. I have read enough, heard enough and experienced enough to know every ounce of the Bible is divinely inspired by the Holy Spirit and is backed by God Almighty. We won't ever figure out all the whys, wheres and whens of Him or His kingdom until we go away to be with Him. To finish this chapter I am going to share many of the words of wisdom Jesus spoke to me in my journaling time. Everything I share is exactly how I heard them while praying in tongues. I do not change any words but copy them directly from my journals. I hope you are blessed in the hearing of these sayings just as I have been.

1. Be at peace for the ways I teach have remained the same. No man recalls his teacher unless he taught him something.
2. I scan this earth looking for the one, the two, the many I may send, that I may send one, two and or many to do my will.
3. Make a way for truth so that truth may make a way.
4. Climb a hill. Climb a mountain. Both are feats for the body. Both are challenges, so therefore one can acclaim victory as one conquers its task.
5. Take a grain of wheat, just one. Look at its possibility. It can be crushed to produce. Add it to many other grains and the possibilities are endless.
6. Treat others with respect so as to be one of credibility. Be known as one who is credible and respectable.
7. Care for the old, for their ways are old. An old way is an old way. But an old man cares for the way of old.
8. Each step man takes is a step in a particular direction, but, when a step is misplaced complacency sets in.
9. It's a gift of God that gives all the ideas that race throughout this earth. Why should a man say it is mine when all is the Lords?
10. Ears do hear but hearts don't receive. Mouths do speak but actions are weak.
11. Truth is present and truth is given. Receive the truth to have and possess full enlightenment.
12. So where shall a man lie? Shall he be in the realm of maximized works or shall he dwell in lethargy? Take a pint of anything. Take a quart of anything. Which would you choose? The larger amount is desirable. Go for the

maximum. Go for the most of all things. Teach others the same thing.

13. A truth is truth. Stand on it. Walk on it. Show it off. Share it. Bring it wherever you go. Give it away.

14. Take My word and bend it into every outlet so that it may go out with power. Take it always with you.

15. Abide by My truth alone for it is truth that will set many free. It has been released to reveal the false. As truth stands beside false, false has to bow. Only as truth stands alongside false will it bow. If false stands alone, it stands until it is revealed.

16. Speak the plain truth. Truth is very exact and is alone truth. It needs nothing else to surround it or crowd it. Truth is simple in nature and is above and below a surface of all things. In an event where truth is not presented the surface is tainted and all that is within is tainted also. That which is seen and that which is unseen is corrupted.

17. There is power in surrender. You forfeit all, yet, you gain all that is on the other side.

18. It is man alone that lies in a kingdom, all his own, for he creates it, dwells in it and falls before it.

19. Give ear to my words that the days may be full and rich and full of my glory. Take each day and dissect it. Which part will carry on and which will go by the wayside? Distinguish between the two and separate yourself from that which is eternal and that which is temporary. (look at them) Cling to the eternal.

20. Space has been given you. Place has been prepared for you and pace has been designed for you. Now, all three are perfect for you. (Place, space and pace) How good it is for you this day. Peace, be still.

21. Deliberate among yourselves to deliberately use the Word of God. It will be the train you ride among many sports cars. None can beat it. None can out power it. It goes according to its course and it stays on course. All else stands back to allow it to run its course. Whole towns are split by it. The course of My word continues throughout time, just as a

train. Its purpose is to <u>carry</u> out the plan of God perfecting the way of the saints.

22. Mountains and valleys are alike in one thing. They both slope one way or another. They are reflective of one another. It takes a strong man to climb a mountain. But, it takes a strong man to climb up out of a valley. To come off of a mountain is like a trip to the valley. It is easy to come down. So, the ways the man can go are many yet, are the same.

23. Respond slowly, yet respond timely

24. A man is appointed to die only once. But, a man who continues to die daily is worthy of his hire.

25. Count your many blessings for they shall increase into great abundance. The foolish shall not receive such an abundance.

26. Relentlessly, time is giving over to the Kingdom with the power thrust of the Lord God Almighty. It has no choice!

27. Knowledge can beat the best of men. Although man thinks he masters knowledge! He is yet to come into the knowledge of God.

28. Be at a place and settle in. Be at a place and busy about. Be at a place and absolutely be still. See, the three of these will make a man completely fulfilled in his place of occupation for there is a time for all things in all places.

29. Selfish pride is one that looks at itself in the mirror and says, "Look what I have done and look what I have!" Love looks in the mirror and says, "Look what the Lord has done and look what I have become!"

30. Hesitate only to disregard the trivial. But, ponder on many ideas that will bring forth a great garden of pleasures.

31. Flee seven directions and come back unprepared. Stay in one spot and receive discipline.

32. There will be a day that kingdoms will rise and kingdoms will fall and yet, My Kingdom has not fallen nor has it risen. For there is no kingdom of Mine that is not and then is, and is, then is not.

33. He who stands under a fallen rock gets crushed. He who dances in my presence gets fullness of joy.

34. My hand is secure and your grip must be secure. Take not security in the things of this world.

35. My ways are frequented by many. But, many frequently miss my ways.

36. An appetite is strongest when one has worked all day and comes in to rest. But My Kingdom is just the opposite. When one hungers he will become a worker. As he hungers he is filled and then it gives him stamina to go out.

37. If a man avails much on his own, then in his mind he needs no God. But, if a man has seen the plan of God in his life, then he will relinquish it unto me.

38. Diligently delight in My Kingdom. See its ways and see its countenance. It is arrayed with beauty and it is full of courtships.

39. Take lies and turn them around to be truth for within a lie there lies truth.

40. Reach out your hand. What do you see? You see nothing. When I reach out My hand what do you see? You see where a sacrifice was made. Something has been removed because it was a sacrifice. When ever sacrifice comes something must go.

41. Ponder on this! Take a piece of bacon and fry it. It reduces in size. Now take the flesh and crucify it and it reduces in size. The heat does the same for both.

42. Tidily winks! Take one to move another. This is how I do with my people.

43. Delight in my ways. Take a child, for instance. You take him to the fair and he wants more. You take him to the zoo and he wants more. But, take him in your arms and see his content.

44. The birds have the sky to fly. The animals roam the earth. But, man shall soar by the Spirit of God.

45. A worn out old shoe can be a good thing, for it is an outward appearance of something that needs repair. But, with a clock, a brokenness that lies within is not easily detected.

46. As one with wisdom of God and one with the wisdom of the Word there can be no mistake of any matter of truth.

47. The wise would take every opportunity to listen to me for one hour and then go on to the second hour.

48. The light has come and so has the day begun.

49. The hand that carries the money needs to take care of the hand that takes charge of the home. And likewise the hand that takes care of the home needs to take care of the hand with the money.

50. Tall trees truly do stand tall. But, does a short stump reap the benefit of what it used to be? I say not! So, don't be a short stump. Be a tall tree.

51. A suitcase can be empty or full. When it's full you are going some place. When it's empty it's stored away. I desire that your suitcase be full; to be ready to go. Read the Word!

52. Speak truth and walk in truth. Don't make up your own truths for your truths are not My truths. Your truths are twisted. They are like unto a pretzel. They are self serving. They come back to self.

53. There is a peach. It falls from the tree and knows from where it comes. Yet, the apple that is thrown under the peach tree is confused. For the apple does not belong to the peach tree. So I say, that when a man comes unto me he knows the way. But if he doesn't come unto me he shall not know of his way.

54. Take this can of soda and shake it. From the outside you can not tell that it has incurred a shaking. No signs are available. But as soon as you open it, there it goes all over the place. Then there is sure evidence of the shaking. This is like a man that has been upset over a matter and then keeps it to himself.

55. A man spends a lifetime in truth or he spends a lifetime trying to survive.

56. Upholding truth makes a man merry in his heart over many matters. Teach others the truths that I bestow. They need to hear the miracles of God and not a few steps of success.

57. The backside of every dish is known of its maker. So shall the earth be turned and be known of its maker.

58. Suffer not the little children. Do not deprive, those lacking in depth of knowledge of the Lord, for the sake of their lack.

59. There is no sign to see when a man is angered and holds onto his tongue. But, when a man is angered and does not hold onto his tongue then it is like a ship that crashes into the shore and becomes shipwrecked. He then can not pull back and work his way out because by his words he is trapped. Do you see?

60. Take a choice given to you and choose wisely. For it is in the choosing that will warrant the success of a thing.

61. Take patience and turn it around and it creates irritation. Take patience and use it and it will bring peace of mind.

62. An ounce of willingness is worth a pound of effort.

Chapter 7
Conclusion

As I come to the final chapter of this book I am reminded of the reason I write it.

Jesus is the same yesterday, today and forever!

As we walk with Jesus and confess Him as being our Lord, there is a great expectancy upon our lives. As we make our Heavenly Father known to the world we must come into alliance with Jesus so we represent the Father as accurately as we are able. Many of us do not really know the God we serve. Long ago, the Lord showed me that I only knew about Him. He said I only knew Him according to what I read and what other people said about Him. The Bible is complete in describing Him and telling all about who He is. However, sometimes this knowing Him remains primarily head knowledge. I have spent the last twenty six years as a Christian but, nothing compares to getting to know Him better by the way of His Spirit. As we read about Him we know Him. But, as we experience Him as a real person, through the Holy Spirit, we get a more complete understanding of who He really is. I would venture to say that it will take all throughout eternity to learn all of His ways. We must walk in the fullness of God to know His ways and to have the ability to introduce Him to this lost world, effectively and accurately. Introducing Him is only the beginning. We must get to know Him, the one in whom we serve. We can only accomplish this by having fellowship with Him and by hearing Him. As we are led by His Spirit we come into alignment with His will.

Romans 8:14(NKJV) *For as many as are led by the Spirit of God, these are sons of God.*

As we see how Jesus walked on this earth, going about doing the Father's business, we must follow His lead. He too was led by the Holy Spirit. To SEE what the Father is doing is a must. Just like Jesus, we have to go about doing our Father's business according to the Word and according to the leading of the Holy Spirit.

Luke 2:49(NKJV) *And He said to them, "Why did you seek Me? Did you not know that I must be about My Father's business?"*

Luke 4:1(NKJV) *Then Jesus, being filled with the Holy Spirit, returned from the Jordan and was led by the Spirit into the wilderness,*

We can not deny the power inside of us. We must <u>acknowledge Him in all of our ways</u>. That is how we represent Him accurately. People have to know Jesus of today and that He has not changed. He still Saves. He still Heals. He still Delivers. He still Speaks to His people. He still gives Dreams and Visions. He still performs Miracles. That's Jesus! That is Jesus of yesterday. That is Jesus today. And that is Jesus forever. Nothing will ever change this description of Him. His people have misrepresented Him, including me. We must pray because many of us lack the ability to represent Him accurately. We must pray for all He has for us and then be faithful to walk in it as completely as we are able. We must begin to pray for wisdom. We must pray to receive the Holy Spirit and be endued with power. If you do not know whether you have been filled with the Holy Spirit since you believed in Christ Jesus, pray that you be filled. We can no longer just lethargically wait for God to do something. He has already done everything and has <u>given us everything</u> we need to move out in obedience, in power and in victory. He is waiting for us to receive and then respond. He's waiting for us to actively seek Him and to seek out all of His ways. As His ways are not like ours, He's looking for those that diligently seek Him for that new way of living. He will reward those who are seekers. We must believe the Word of God and exercise the giftings that He has placed in us by His Spirit. We have to use **everything,** He has given us. Here is one more story the Lord told me. It describes and illustrates perfectly what I am trying to say.

Use All God Has Given

I saw a ladybug crawl up a huge wall. He began to climb and climb. He said, "God would never have me climb up this wall because it is too hard and is too long of a journey." So the ladybug climbed back down off the wall. Then he ran right into God. God pointed at the wall and said, "I told you to go up that wall." The ladybug shook his head in total disbelief and said, "God would not ask me to climb that wall because it is too hard and too long of a journey." He then walked away and *spread his wings and flew away.*

The Lord said, "If my people would use all that I have given them, the journey would not be as long and as hard.

I have a great hope to live out the ways of the Bible, using what God has given and manifesting God's presence. We are all ladybugs to varying degrees. Sometimes we just don't know what we have and who we are as believers. Press toward the mark for the prize of that High Calling. Use what ever you have been given and soar to great heights with Him.

Philippians 3:14-16(NKJV) I press toward the goal for the prize of the upward call of God in Christ Jesus. Therefore let us, as many as are mature, have this mind; and if in anything you think otherwise, God will reveal even this to you. Nevertheless, to the degree that we have already attained, let us walk by the same rule, let us be of the same mind.

Instead of allowing the world to proclaim that people can know things because they are psychic, we must proclaim **the prophetic** in activity. We must let people know the Lord speaks by His Holy Spirit and His people hear His voice. We must be bold and be confident in revealing the true attributes of God.

The Lord showed me a vivid vision one time. I saw a room full of people. The people of God were whispering to one another about God. During this vision the Lord spoke and said to stop this whispering. Finally, the people began talking in a normal voice about the things of God. As other people heard things about God, they too began to whisper. Again, He rose up and said STOP WHISPERING!

The enemy wants us to whisper. He wants us to be quiet about the things of God because he knows what will happen if the whole truth about the Lord is revealed. This world, assuredly, will be turned upside down by the manifest presence of God. Prepare the way of the Lord!

This generation is looking for something to believe in and they take notice of the miraculous. Our God is miraculous. All that He represents is beyond miraculous. Therefore we must come into agreement with the Word, not denying the power that dwells in us by the Holy Spirit. Tell the world! Be open about ALL He is! We have to look at the examples set before us in the Word and begin to pray for those manifestations of the Holy Spirit because that is who He is. Use what God gives to its fullest potential. As our mouths have been closed, people have remained ignorant of the true ways of God. We have dummied down the Word. It has kept the saved and the unsaved **ignorant** of who Jesus is and what His kingdom is about. We have kept it comfortable, instead of life changing. We must pray for all the giftings because as they operate in us, we will come out of our natural fleshly selves and be more like Jesus. He ministered by the Holy Spirit and we must also. We must minister in power. The gospel does not come in word only but it comes in POWER also.

> *1 Thessalonians 1:5(NKJV) For our gospel did not come to you in word only, **but also in power,** and in the Holy Spirit and in much assurance, as you know what kind of men we were among you for your sake.*

Somewhere we have lost the way of the God of the Bible. We have to be the New Testament Church to get the New Testament Church results! If he tells us to listen to Him and not harden our hearts then He must be a speaking God and we obviously have, consistently throughout time, had a heart problem. Pray that your heart be open to the things of God no matter how it goes against past teachings or traditional religious ways. Pray in tongues more than anyone else and then pray that you will interpret for understanding. Break out of your self-made box and walk in the freedom and liberty of the Spirit, gaining balance and maturity.

Let this world see the manifestations of God. The enemy does not want us to tell the whole truth about Jesus because he knows **people will become dangerous to him.** I find that some Christians barely believe in healing nor do they believe in deliverance from demons. Jesus ministered in healing and deliverance and we are to do these things likewise. There are great treasures for us to uncover in God's Kingdom. The Lord calls us His peculiar treasure. We have immense treasures inside of us because of His deposited Holy Spirit. He also says that in the house of the righteous there is much treasure. I am looking for the treasures He has hidden. The more I dig the more I seem to find.

Matthew 13:44(NKJV) *"Again, the kingdom of heaven is like treasure hidden in a field, which a man found and hid; and for joy over it he goes and sells all that he has and buys that field.*

Here is something He told me about treasure a couple of weeks ago. As we are open to more of Jesus, He has more for us to turn and reveal to the rest of the world. What treasure can you find?

A treasure is like this. It is something that many seek after, yet rarely find. Treasure upon this earth is hidden and can be found. My treasure is for the righteous and for the upright. Some come upon the treasure but squander it on useless devices. My treasure is found in very unlikely places. It is found in the stillness of the night. It is found in the sweet whispers of My voice. So as a man listens and is quiet and has an ear to hear, so he may be the one that is wealthiest of all!

Jesus brings salvation to a lost world. We have to present Him as OUR SAVIOR. Furthermore, we must not forget the rest of the inheritance that goes with being a child of the King. His Kingdom is endless with possibilities of laying hands on the sick so they may recover, laying hands on those to receive the Holy Spirit, and laying hands on people to impart spiritual gifts. We can speak with new tongues and pray to interpret tongues. We can prophecy and have great faith to do miracles. If David danced, pray that you will dance. If Solomon received great wisdom from God, pray that you too will have great wisdom. If Paul had visions and dreams, then pray for the dreams and visions. If Peter led hundreds to the Lord then pray that you will too. If the disciples prayed for people to be delivered of the demonic and healed of their infirmities, then do these things. *If it is in the Bible*, it is ours to be had. If it is exampled in the Word there is absolutely nothing keeping us from it. We have to <u>perpetuate a motion and cause a commotion</u> in this earth. Jesus did! Join me by spreading *all the news* of a Mighty God who sent His Precious Son which in turn sent us the Holy Spirit. Make a great proclamation to move forward in great power giving all glory to Him!

Let's all hear, someday, these words…Well done good and faithful servant!

Matthew 25:23(NKJV)

His lord said to him, 'Well done, good and faithful servant; you have been faithful over a few things, I will make you ruler over many things. Enter into the joy of your lord.'

About the Author

Shirley Hall has been an educator in the public school system for over twenty years. She is married and has three grown children. She has a heart for woman and has ministered many years to women in solitary confinement in a correctional institute. She is an intercessor and has received much of her revelation from the Lord through journaling and from dreams and visions. Under the direction of the Holy Spirit she authored "The Voice of God" A Church with Hearing Ears, and has written several children's books.

LaVergne, TN USA
03 August 2010
191882LV00005B/2/P